Travellers

MAINLAND GREECE
INCLUDING ATHENS

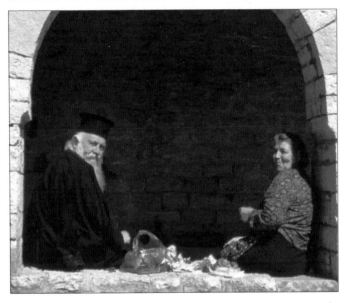

BY
ROBIN GAULDIE

Produced by
Thomas Cook Publishing

Written by Robin Gauldie
Original photography by Terry Harris

Edited and designed by Laburnum Technologies Pvt Ltd,
C-533 Triveni Apts, Sheikh Sarai Phase 1,
New Delhi 110017

Published by Thomas Cook Publishing
A division of Thomas Cook Tour Operations Limited

PO Box 227, Unit 15/16, Coningsby Road,
Peterborough PE3 8SB, United Kingdom.
E-mail: books@thomascook.com www.thomascookpublishing.com

ISBN: 1-841573-82-5

First edition © 2004 Thomas Cook Publishing

Head of Thomas Cook Publishing: Donald Greig
Project Editor: Charlotte Christensen
Project Administrator: Michelle Warrington
DTP: Steven Collins

Series Manager: Stephen York

Printed and bound in Spain by: Grafo Industrias Graficas, Basauri

Cover: Portico of the caryatids on the Eréchtheion
Photograph by: Guy Thouvenin/Robert Harding World Imagery
Inside cover: photographs supplied by Spectrum Colour Library

CD manufacturing services provided by: business interactive ltd,
Rutland, UK
CD edited and designed by: Laburnum Technologies Pvt Ltd

Contents

Introduction

Greece is where the distant past and the vital present meet; a land of big cities and empty hillsides, snow-capped peaks and sandy beaches, ancient temples and busy summer holiday resorts. No other European country has such deep cultural roots, tapping into more than 4,000 years of Hellenic history – and few other European countries offer such a variety of things to do and places to see.

Spectacular soaring rocks of Metéora village

Apart from its ancient archaeological sites, mainland Greece offers some of the last wilderness areas and uncrowded beaches in Europe, many of them unknown to the millions who visit the Greek islands each year.

Though most Greeks have abandoned their colourful traditional costumes, the country's folklore still comes to life during the many summer festivals and saints' days, when Greeks celebrate with hearty feasting, boisterous music and dancing.

Life is lived outdoors most of the year, and there is nothing to beat sitting at a shady harbour-side table eating freshly caught fish or octopus, with a glass of ice-cold beer or a carafe of strong-tasting *retsina*. Food in Greece is simple – and relatively cheap.

In addition to fine beaches, Greece offers ancient cities, lost temples,

Fishing boats at Astakos

Mainland Greece

crusader castles and mighty sea fortresses amid striking scenery. You can choose from bright, modern apartments and small hotels to live in, bustling resorts, or finely restored traditional mansions, castles or former monasteries.

Lovers of nature will find isolated mountain wildernesses and giant freshwater lakes which attract Europe's rarest birds, and fields and forests full of wild flowers and dazzling butterflies.

For those in search of sport, Greece offers the best yachting and windsurfing in Europe, plus waterskiing from dozens of sunny beaches, parascending, diving

and snorkelling. Few other countries pack such an array of delights into such a small space.

The Land

Mainland Greece covers some 130,000 sq km. To the west, the Adriatic separates it from Italy. To the south lies the Mediterranean and to the east are the Aegean and its islands. Greece has some of the most spectacular landscapes and wide open spaces in Europe, from the peaks of Ólimbos (Olympus) to the rolling farmlands of Thrace.

The barren rocks of the *kástro* at Monemvasía

Much of the country is mountainous, and throughout history the mountains have provided a defence against invasion and a refuge for those resisting occupying powers. Wherever you are in Greece there are mountains on the horizon, and you are never more than a few hours' drive from the sea.

Economy and Population

Greece has a population of almost 11 million, 3.2 million of whom live in and around Athens. More than one in four Greeks work on the land, many of them on small, family-owned farms, and almost half are self-employed. It is still a fairly poor country, and many people hold down several jobs in order to make ends meet. Money sent home by Greeks living overseas provides invaluable help to many families.

Farming

Oranges and lemons, cotton, tobacco, grapes and, above all, olives grow in abundance in the fertile valleys and plains and are among the country's major exports. Sheep and goats graze on higher, barren ground.

Flora and Fauna

Though intensive farming has taken its toll of Greek wildlife, low population density has left niches for many rare and endangered species (*see pp138–9*).

Geology and Climate

Beneath the thin topsoil, most of Greece is porous limestone. Water drains through it quickly, giving mountains and hillsides a parched, near-desert look for much of the year. Underground rivers have cut through the rock in many places, creating echoing caverns lined with coloured spires and stalactites. Topsoil washed from the mountainsides has accumulated over millennia in fertile valleys watered by rivers which swell with winter rains and melting snow but dwindle to a trickle in the hot summers. Winters are short, mild and wet on the plains and around the coasts, but can be bitterly cold in the mountains.

The Sea

If the mountains defend and divide Greece, the sea unites it with the outside world and provides a living for thousands of sailors and fishermen. The Greek merchant navy is one of the world's biggest and rivals tourism as the country's biggest foreign currency earner and one of its biggest employers.

In ancient times the sea linked the enterprising Greeks with the great empires of the Middle East, and adventurous mariners from the Greek city-states founded colonies as far afield as Marseilles and Sicily in the west and the shores of the Black Sea in the east. Well into this century it was easier to travel by sea than by road and little mainland ports like Yíthion, Neapoli or Yerolimín were thriving centres of import and export to Athens and abroad. Much of their trade now goes by road, and these sleepy, forgotten harbours with their rows of merchants' mansions are some of the pleasantest places in which to spend a Greek holiday.

Environment

Greece's record on the environment could be better. Local authorities have neither the money nor the powers to clean up the mess, and the national government in Athens has yet to show any real interest in doing so. Interference from abroad is widely resented, and Greeks often argue that the tourists who complain about litter-strewn beaches are the very people who create the litter.

Less obvious to the holiday visitor is the environmental damage being inadvertently caused by misdirected European Union investment. Greece, the poorest country in the EU, is a major beneficiary of its regional funds, and Greek farmers have been quick to see the benefits of the EU's agricultural subsidy system. On the mainland, tobacco and cotton cultivation is booming as never before and a European glut of both crops means farmers are paid to plough them back into the soil. The farmers can hardly be blamed for trying to make easy money, but the consequences are worrying. Many of Greece's rivers have been reduced to a mere trickle by dams built to meet the country's fast-growing need for hydroelectric power. At their mouths, delta wetlands, which shelter thousands of rare birds, are being drained by tobacco and cotton farmers. Greece's longest and mightiest river, the Akhelóös (see p94), is threatened by a new set of dams which will cut off water from the wetlands at its mouth, drown a remote and historic monastery and village in the Píndhos mountains, and cut off water from existing dams down river. Ironically, the EU, which is backing the multi-million ECU project, has already prosecuted Greece in the European Court for failing to protect these very same wetlands that the dam threatens.

The northern Pindhos mountain range, a surviving area of wilderness in southern Europe

History

BC	
1700–1600	Mycenaean culture emerges on mainland.
1200	Collapse of Mycenaean culture.
1100	Arrival of the Dorian Greeks.
776	First Olympic Games.
800–600	City-state system emerges.
490	First Persian invasion. Athenian victory at the battle of Marathon.
480	Second Persian invasion. Greek army annihilated at Thermopylae, and Athens captured. Persian navy defeated at Salamis.
479	Persians defeated at Plataiai and Mycale. End of the Persian Wars.
478	Athens at the height of its power as leader of the Delian League.
431–404	Peloponnesian War between Sparta and Athens ending in Athenian defeat.
371	Thebes defeats Sparta at the Battle of Lévktra.

359–336	Rise of Macedonia.
338	Macedonia defeats southern cities at Battle of Khairónia.
336–323	Reign of Alexander the Great.
323–196	Macedonian kings.
200–146	Wars with Rome, culminating in the end of Greek and Macedonian independence.
AD 242–251	Goths appear on the Greek frontier for the first time.
324	The Roman Emperor Constantine moves his capital to Byzantium (Istanbul), renaming it Constantinople and founding the Christian (Byzantine) empire in Greece and the east.
393	Olympic Games banned by the Roman Emperor Theodosius.
529	Last schools of philosophy suppressed in Athens.
600–700	Pagan Slavs and Goths invade Greece as far as the Peloponnese.

800–900	Byzantine recovery.
1204	Frankish/Venetian Fourth Crusade sacks Constantinople and divides Greece.
1261–2	Byzantine Empire recovers Constantinople and most of mainland Greece.
1354	Ottoman Turks capture Gallipoli.
1429	Turks take Thessaloníki.
1453	Fall of Constantinople and the end of the Byzantine Empire.
1499	Turks take Návpaktos, Koróni and Methóni from Venice.
1537–40	Turks take Monemvasía and Návplion.
1571	Turks checked at Battle of Lepanto by Holy League led by Austrian Don John.
1685–99	Venice recovers the Peloponnese.
1821–30	War of Independence. The Peloponnese, Athens and Attica, Sterea Ellas, the Cyclades and the Argo-Saronic islands

	become the new Republic of Greece.
1831	President Capodistrias assassinated.
1833	Bavarian Prince Otto becomes King Otho I of the Hellenes.
1881	Turkey cedes Thessaly to Greece.
1912	First Balkan War. Greece gains Thessaloniki, Ionina and Epirus from Turkey.
1913	Second Balkan War. Greece allied with Serbia against Bulgaria.
1917	Greece joins Britain and France in World War I.
1919	Greece lands troops at Smyrna (Izmir) in Turkey.
1920–23	War between Greece and Turkey ends in defeat for Greece. Around 1 million Greeks driven from Turkey; 400,000 Muslims driven out of Greece.

War of Independence helmet

1924–36	Political chaos, leading to suspension of constitution. General Metaxas becomes dictator.	**1974**	Collapse of the junta after the Turkish invasion of Cyprus. Restoration of democracy.
1939	Italy invades Albania.	**1981**	Greece joins the European Community. Left-wing PASOK led by Andreas Papandreou elected.
1940	Italy demands access to Greek ports. Metaxas refuses. Italian invasion defeated in Epirus.		
1941–4	German occupation. Varied resistance groups active in many areas, including growing Communist faction.	**1989**	PASOK defeated. Series of short-lived caretaker governments.
		1993	PASOK re-elected.
1946–9	Civil war.	**1996**	Costas Simitis elected Prime Minister.
1967–74	Military junta rules Greece, led by Colonel Papadopoulos. King Constantine expelled. Referendum ends the monarchy.	**1997**	Athens chosen to host the 2004 Olympics.
		2000	PASOK re-elected.
		2003	Greece adopts the euro.

Empires, Hegemonies and Invasions
The Mycenaeans and Dorians

The Mycenaean Bronze Age warriors built citadels ringed by massive boulder walls in the Peloponnese, Athens, Thebes and elsewhere, and traded with Egypt and the empires of the Middle East. Their civilisation toppled around 1200 BC. About 150 years later, the first Greek-speaking, iron-using Dorians arrived from the north, settled among the ruins of the Mycenaean civilisation, and over the next 300 years developed their own culture.

The City-states

By the 8th century BC Greece was divided into dozens of small, fiercely independent city-states. Not all were Athenian-style democracies. Sparta was an authoritarian, militarised state ruled by two kings. Other cities were democracies, oligarchies controlled by a group of powerful men, or tyrannies under an absolute ruler. The rival cities banded together against Persia in the early 5th century BC, but after the invasion Athens and Sparta fought each other for almost 30 years. Sparta, the victor in 404 BC, was in turn defeated by Thebes, which dominated Greece until the rise of Macedonia (*see p132*).

The Macedonians and Hellenistic Greece

Macedonia and a number of smaller kingdoms created by Alexander's generals dominated the Greek world from the end of the 4th century BC until the Roman conquest. Other Hellenistic kingdoms were created in the Middle East, giving the Greeks broader horizons. Despite political chaos and frequent conflict among Alexander's successors, trade, philosophy and the arts flourished in the wider Greek world, but the mainland cities stagnated.

The Romans in Greece

Roman legions first landed in Greece in 201 BC. Over the next century Rome became increasingly powerful and was frequently at war with Macedonia. Greek cities which resisted Roman hegemony were destroyed, as Corinth was in 146 BC. The Roman conquest was completed in 86 BC when Athens fell, bringing almost three centuries of stability, during which Athens flourished with the building of a new Roman city beside the ancient Greek one. Corinth, too, was rebuilt and in the later Roman period Thessaloníki became a great trade centre.

The Byzantine Empire

In AD 330 the Roman Emperor Constantine dedicated his new capital of Byzantium (now Istanbul) and renamed it Constantinople. The city became the heart of a Christian empire which was more Greek than Roman, with territory which included all of Greece and Asia Minor and much of the Middle East. It lasted for more than 1,000 years, withstanding invasions by Slavs, Bulgars, Persians, Saracens and Turks until its final defeat in 1453.

The Venetians

Venice, with its eyes on the Greek islands, encouraged its Frankish allies of the Fourth Crusade to sack Constantinople in 1204. The Venetians then seized Évvoia (Evia), the Ionian islands and strategic harbours throughout Greece. When Constantinople fell to the Turks, the Venetians held on to mainland and island strongholds including Monemvasía, Methóni and Koróni, Návplion, Návpaktos, Rion and Andírrion, and as late as the end of the 17th century reconquered most of the Peloponnese from Turkey before being finally driven out of the mainland for good in 1715.

The Turks in Greece

The Turkish conquest cut Greece off from the Christian West but made it part of a vast Muslim Ottoman empire. The seafaring Greeks carried on much of the trade of this empire, and Greek traders and shipbuilders flourished. The Turks tolerated other religions but punished rebellion with extreme ferocity. Despite this, risings against the Turks were frequent. In 1821 a final struggle for independence began, leading to the creation of the first independent Greek state in 1830.

Governance

Politics is a favourite topic of Greek conversation. Memories of the 1946–9 Civil War and of the 1967–74 military junta have begun to fade, but political discussion is guaranteed to raise voices and tempers and the fiercest debate is often between those who are on the same side. In 1993 passionate protest followed the unofficial visit of ex-king Constantine, who had been rejected in the referendum of 1973. Since 1974, Greece has been a parliamentary democracy with an elected president whose role is mainly ceremonial. Real power is in the hands of an elected prime minister. The next elections are due to be held in 2004.

Campaign posters flash pictures of political leaders

Political Parties

Two major parties dominate Greek politics. PASOK, a left-wing alliance, ruled through much of the 1980 and 1990s, and is still in power at the time of writing. The aggressively right-wing Nea Dimokratia (New Democracy) party, in power between 1990 and 1993, made itself unpopular by a wide-ranging programme of privatisation of state enterprises and a drive to collect tax from a workforce which is nearly 50 per cent self-employed.

Nea Dimokratia was toppled by the defection of one of its ministers, Antonios Samaras, whose Politiki Anoikti (Political Spring) party campaigned on a fiercely nationalist platform to win a handful of seats.

Two other minority parties, the old-style KKE (Greek Communist Party) and a reformed socialist party, are also represented in the national parliament.

Greece and Europe

Anything touching on Greece's hard-won sovereignty quickly becomes a hot political issue, often overshadowing rational discussion of the shaky state of the Greek economy – partly kept afloat by the European Union – which has urged Greece to privatise its

THE COLONELS' JUNTA

On 21 April 1967 a group of army officers staged a coup d'état to prevent the election of a left-wing government. The junta, led by Colonel Yioryios Papadopoulos, censored the press, banned trade unions, imprisoned thousands of opponents and banned free speech, popular music, short skirts, long hair and beards. Despite this mixture of terror and petty stupidity, the colonels were strongly supported by the USA, and many Greeks believe their coup was a CIA plot. The junta fell in 1974 after its backing for a right-wing Greek coup in Cyprus led to Turkish invasion of the island.

unwieldy nationalised enterprises and reduce a huge economic deficit. Modernisation measures (including higher taxes) are widely disliked and universally blamed on Brussels, but many Greeks seem able to ignore the visible benefits of EU membership.

The PASOK government, which was stridently anti-American during its first two terms, began its third spell in office with peace overtures towards the USA, partly to balance grass-roots anti-European feeling.

Neighbouring Turkey, though a NATO ally, is still seen as a threat, and Greece spends proportionately more on defence than any other European country. Relations between the two countries are strained mainly due to the situation in Cyprus. However, when Turkey suffered a terrible earthquake in 1999, Greece was the first country to send in humanitarian aid.

The hottest issue in recent years has been Macedonia – a name to which Greece claims sole rights but which is also claimed by the former Yugoslav republic across the border. Greek ministers refuse to recognise the newly independent state under that name, referring to it instead as the Republic of Skopje (after its capital) or as FYROM, an acronym for Former Yugoslav Republic of Macedonia. The recognition of the former Yugoslav republic by European nations in 1993 brought loud protest from Greece, but in 1995, Greece also recognised FYROM.

Vouli (parliament building) in Athens

Politics and Philosophy

'. . . Plato points upward to heaven, Aristotle downward to the earth.'
CLEMENT CJ WEBB, *A History of Philosophy*, Oxford University Press, 1915

Athens was the most democratic of
the Greek city-states, but it was a
strictly limited democracy. Only free men
born in the city might vote, and even at
the best of times the man in the street
might be more easily inspired by
charismatic orators than by level-headed
statesmen.

Philosophical debate was as intense as
political argument, and the philosophers
who entered political discussion are
those best known today.

The philosophers who took an active
part in the political life of the city are
nevertheless outnumbered by those who
stood aloof from it, preferring the
discussion of ideals to realities. In fact,
the schools of Hellenic philosophy
flowered in the 4th and 3rd centuries

BC, when Athens was no longer the
greatest power in the Greek world, and
many of the most influential teachers
argued for individual self-sufficiency
rather than engagement with the fickle
world. To the Ancient Greeks, 'philosopher' meant no more than 'lover of
knowledge', and philosophy embraced
the entire realm of thought from pure
mathematics to morality and ethics.

Aristotle (843–322 BC)

The tutor of Alexander the Great and
pupil of Plato (his name means 'the best
student'), he is the least mystical of the
Greeks and arguably the most influential
on later Western thinkers. Much of his
rigorously logical thinking aimed to
explain organic and physical
phenomena; today, he might be a
physicist rather than a philosopher.

Democritus (c.460–c.370 BC)

A contemporary of Plato, Democritus
argued that the world could not be
perceived through the senses alone but
must be understood intellectually. He
conceived the universe as consisting of
tiny, indestructible units, for which he
coined the term 'atoms'.

Diogenes of Sinope
(c.410–c.320 BC)

Founder of the school of philosophers

called the Cynics, Diogenes might be called the first drop-out. He argued for the simple life and rejected the everyday demands of convention, owned as little as possible and lived in a barrel.

Epicurus (341–270 BC)

Epicurus and his followers argued that there is no after-life and that happiness in this one is the chief good, and, therefore, the only reasonable aim.

Plato (427–347 BC)

Plato is among the best-known of all the Greek philosophers, not only because he was the most prolific writer but because so many of his writings have survived. His central argument was that deeper nature and the meaning of things could be determined only by thought, not through the senses.

Socrates (469–399 BC)

Socrates lived and taught when Athens was at its zenith, paving the way for all those who came after him. He left no writings of his own, but is known to us through the work of his followers Plato and Xenophon, and his opponent the playwright Aristophanes, who caricatured him in his play *The Clouds*. His championing of reason over superstition and his delight in argument for its own

sake made him many enemies among Athenian conservatives, who ultimately succeeded in having him tried and convicted on a charge of corrupting Athenian youth. The penalty was death by poison. Socrates might have escaped execution by pleading guilty, but refused to do so.

Zeno of Citium (334–262 BC)

Zeno and his followers, the Stoics (who take their name from the *stoa* or porch of the market-place where they gathered), held that the world was ordered by a divine reason, and Stoic influences are apparent in Christianity. Both Stoics and Cynics were more concerned with finding a philosophy suited to everyday life than with ultimate truths, and the debate which they started continues, one way or another, today.

Facing page: statue of Greek philosopher Aristotle
Below: the death of Socrates, by Jacques-Louis David (19th century)

Culture

Visitors to Greece only a quarter of a century ago might have seen grain being threshed on a stone threshing-floor, taken to the mill by mules, ground by wind power and baked in a wood-fired village oven. Greece has come a long way since then. Mules are still useful load carriers all over the country, but they are no longer the lifeline of many villages. New roads and shiny pick-up trucks are the signs of a new prosperity.

Windows on the World

Television, no longer an unattainable luxury, is a fixture in most Greek homes. Video and satellite TV have turned out-of-the-way hamlets into suburbs of the global information village.

Taverna-owners who used to add up the bill on the paper tablecloth or the back of a cigarette packet are now just as likely to use a brand-new personal computer, and although it can take up to two years to have a telephone installed, many shepherds and villagers find cheap mobile phones a convenient substitute.

Fishermen, a mainstay of Greece's economy, also benefit from new technology, and most of the larger vessels have ship-to-shore radio and radar.

The Tourism Boom

Transport within Greece has become faster and more efficient. Perhaps even more importantly, for a country cut off by sea and international politics from its Western European trading partners, international transport links have improved. Holiday jets bring millions of tourists into Athens and other mainland airports at Kalamata, Préveza and Thessaloníki, but they also take Greeks abroad.

Change for the Better?

Not all the changes have been positive – at least from the visitor's point of view. Those seeking tranquillity will be disappointed by the national fondness for massively amplified music and unsilenced motor-

THOMAS COOK'S GREECE

Thomas Cook first visited Greece as part of a tour to the Nile, Palestine, Turkey and Italy in 1869; the party visited Epirus to see the ruins. By 1870 Athens was included in many of Cook's tours and an office was opened in Athens in Place Royale (now Platia Sindagma) in 1883. The building of Greek railways and interest aroused by archaeological excavations ensured a constant stream of customers for Cook's Greek tours to the Grecian islands. The restarting of the original Olympic Games in Athens in 1896 also attracted many visitors. The first conducted tour to Greece took place in 1904.

cycles, and the microwave oven has done more to undermine the reputation of Greek cooking than oil or garlic ever could. Traffic in Athens has grown worse with more widespread car ownership.

Having said that, however, Greece is still a wonderful place in which to get away from it all, and much of the country remains completely unspoilt.

The Greeks Abroad
During the 19th century millions of Greeks emigrated. There are large Greek communities in the USA, Canada, Australia and South Africa, all of them aiming to strike it rich and return home. Visitors who have seen hard-working expatriate Greeks in action may be surprised by how laid-back they seem to be in Greece.

A brighter future for Greece has also encouraged many younger overseas Greeks to return, often bringing fresh ideas and initiatives to the conservative villages their grandparents left. Many young men are put off by the prospect of a spell in uniform. All Greek men must spend 12 months in the armed forces on turning 19, as part of military service.

The company of contemporaries

Pack-mules still carry heavy loads in villages all over Greece

Other Greeks have returned to the land of their ancestors after an even longer absence. As early as the 4th century BC, Greeks had settled on the shores of the Black Sea. With the fall of the Byzantine Empire, they preferred the rule of a Russian Orthodox tsar to that of an Ottoman Muslim sultan. Until the collapse of the USSR, 400,000 Greeks lived in the Soviet republics, many of whom have now chosen to live in Greece.

Greek Personality
You may well meet an Aristotle (Aristotelis) in the corner store or find that your waiter's name is Socrates, but modern Greeks seem to have surprisingly little in common with their heroic ancestors.

There is still a real pride in their achievements, and today's Greeks have inherited the philosopher's delight in ideas and debate, but 2,500 years of change separate them from the builders of the Parthenon. On first acquaintance, Greeks may seem indifferent one moment and pushy the next, but they become firm friends more quickly than any people in Europe.

Festivals

The dates of many Greek festivals are set by the Orthodox calendar, and most of them celebrate one of the hundreds of Orthodox saints, some of them familiar in the West, some of them unique to the Orthodox Church. Many of the festivals are more or less private family affairs, with church services followed by a special meal served at home, but some are bigger and more public celebrations with parades, fireworks and public feasts in which the whole community may join.

Traditional dress for Independence Day

Because so many Greek village families have been separated by migration to the cities or overseas, the biggest and most emotional celebrations are those like the Assumption of the Virgin Mary when all the members of the scattered family return to their ancestral home.

1 January
Áyios Vassilios (St Basil), the Greek equivalent of Santa Claus, comes not on Christmas Day but New Year's Day.

6 January
Epiphany is mainly a religious festival when village wells, springs and the baptismal font of the village church are blessed. At some seaside locations young men traditionally dive for a blessed crucifix, but this custom is dying out.

25 March
The **Feast of the Annunciation** is also celebrated as Independence Day (a bit prematurely as the date marks the beginning of the War of Independence in 1821, not the eventual recovery of all

the territories of modern Greece more than a century later).

April
The three-week period of **Lent** is marked by feasting, carnival and parades, reaching a peak seven weeks before Easter (*see pp20–21*). The biggest and noisiest celebrations are at Patras, where the carnival features a fancy-dress parade, dancing and music. There are celebrations and events too in Athens and Thessaloníki.

23 April
Áyios Yioryios (St George), the patron saint of shepherds, is honoured at village churches in the Píndhos mountains and elsewhere. One of the more accessible celebrations is at Arákhova, on the slopes of Parnassós.

April-May
Make your arrangements well in advance if you plan an Easter visit as all of Greece – and Greeks from all over the world – converge on their family's

village and transport and accommodation are at a premium. **Easter** in Greece is celebrated according to the Orthodox calendar and can be up to three weeks ahead of or behind Easter in the West. Exact dates for Easter and other moveable feasts can be obtained each year from the Greek National Tourist Office (*see p189*).

1 May

May Day is both a traditional holiday on which people gather armfuls of brightly coloured wild flowers to make wreaths which hang above the door until midsummer, and a day of celebration and demonstration for Greece's strong left-wing parties.

18–19 July

Profitis Ilias (the Prophet Elijah) is honoured at his chapel on the highest peak of Taïyetos and at other mountain chapels.

15 August

Apokimisis tis PanÁyias (Assumption of the Virgin) is second only to Easter in importance. Transport and accommodation can be hard to find, because Greeks return to the family village not only from the cities but from overseas. It is a great family celebration, with food, drink and dancing often until daybreak, and well-behaved visitors will be made welcome.

26 October

Áyios Dhimitrios (St Demetrius), patron saint of Thessaloníki, is celebrated here and elsewhere with extensive sampling of the first of the summer wine.

28 October

Only the Greeks could celebrate as a national holiday their entry into a war which devastated their country, but celebrate it they do on **Ochi Day**. It commemorates General Ioannis Metaxas's laconic negative response to the Italian ultimatum of 1940 – 'Ochi' ('No') (*see p111*). Parades, music and dancing mark the event.

25 December

Christmas in Greece is not the major festival or commercial event that it is elsewhere. It is an important religious occasion and is marked by special church services, but there is little public celebration.

31 December

Children traditionally make the rounds of the village or neighbourhood singing carols, and adults get together with neighbours or family.

Celebrating one of Greece's many Orthodox festivals

Easter in a Greek village is a never-to-be-forgotten experience. The biggest event of a crowded festival calendar, it combines solemn religious ceremony, emotional family reunions, and plenty of public song and dance. Most Greek festivals are first and foremost family affairs, celebrated in the home, but Easter spills out into village streets and cafés. With the weather often at its best, and everyone in a holiday mood, Easter is a great time to visit. Winter is over, and the busy summer season has not begun.

For Greeks living abroad, it is a time to go back to their roots. For their children, brought up in the USA, Canada or Australia, it may be the first taste of the very different lifestyle of a Greek village.

A far less commercial event than Christmas in English-speaking countries, Easter is impossible to avoid. The week's sacred events at cathedrals and churches throughout Greece are broadcast continuously on radio and television, and you will hear the solemn Gregorian chants of the Orthodox Church issuing from every place of worship. Bishops and priests abandon their everyday black for the gorgeous, gold-encrusted robes and jewelled crowns worn only for the most sacred occasions. In many places, ancient icons are carried in procession, and outside the churches the air is heavy with incense. Public worship begins on the evening of Good Friday and reaches a climax the following day with midnight mass, the lighting of thousands of candles to reaffirm the Resurrection, and an eruption of fireworks. Easter Sunday traditionally begins with the breaking of the Lenten fast and a lamb or goat is roasted whole for Sunday lunch. Traditionally, red-dyed hard-boiled eggs are handed out as a special Easter delicacy. Merry-making continues through the day and late into the night. Village-wide hangovers on Monday morning are not uncommon.

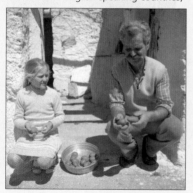

Easter is a mixed time of sombre religious ceremonies (facing page) and boisterous family gatherings. Red-dyed eggs (left) are a special Easter treat

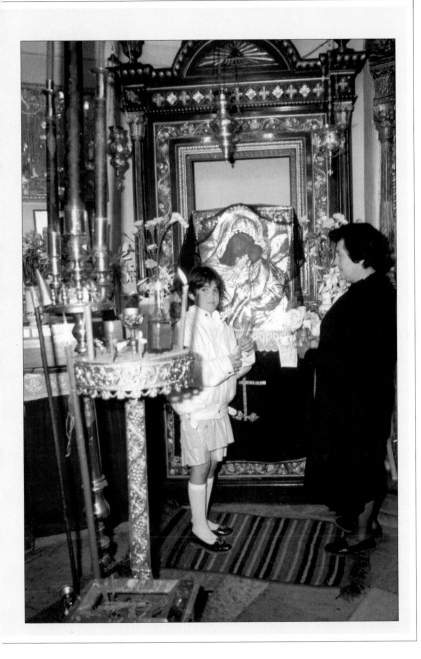

Impressions

Greek hospitality is legendary. Traditionally, any stranger is a guest. That attitude of *philoxenia* ('love of guests') is dying hard with the growth of tourism, but it quickly starts to show itself as you travel away from the busy resorts – or even in them at less busy times of the year. A gift of a flower from someone's garden, nuts or fruit from an orchard you pass, or a carafe of wine sent to your table by a complete stranger comes as a surprise to visitors from less warm-hearted lands.

Street musicians entertain passers-by

Queuing

Queuing for public transport is virtually unheard of, and you must expect a certain amount of pushing and shoving on boarding boats, trains and urban buses. In banks and post offices, however, there is usually a fairly orderly queue – though if you do not step forward promptly when it is your turn, somebody else will.

Dress Code

Topless sunbathing is now accepted on even the most public beaches, but total nudity will offend and may get you arrested. Shorts and T-shirts are acceptable summer wear everywhere except on visits to monasteries and churches, where men must wear long trousers, women skirts which cover the knees, and both sexes should wear long sleeves.

Women Travellers

Greece is still a male-dominated society (though it is changing) but many women feel less risk of harassment than in many other Mediterranean countries. Greek men certainly feel that a woman can only be flattered by their attention, but are unlikely to persist in the face of an unambiguous 'no'. You are more likely to meet with unwanted attention in summer resorts – from summer visitors – than from local people elsewhere.

Language

The Greek language can be intimidating, if only because its alphabet is so different from the familiar Roman script, but a little Greek goes a very long way in making friends and influencing people. Greeks firmly believe that their language is almost impossible for foreigners to learn, and even knowledge of a few simple phrases will be admired and extravagantly praised.

Greeks use a lot of body language (they say that to silence a Greek you need only tie his hands behind his back) which can be helpful and confusing by turns. One helpful hint: a backward jerk of the head which you might interpret as a nod is exactly the opposite. Often accompanied by a click of the tongue, it means 'no'. On the other hand, a rapid side-to-side shake of the head is not a negative – it could mean anything from 'I don't understand' to 'What can I do for you?'

The Greek alphabet is impossible to translate directly into other languages, and vice versa: it takes quite a while to puzzle out that *xampourgker* means 'hamburger' or *kroyasan* means 'croissant'. Some Roman letters are missing from the Greek alphabet, and are represented by combining two Greek letters to make the appropriate sound. *Mu* and *pi* are combined to make a hard B as in bar; *nu* and *taf* to make a hard D as in dog; and *nu* and *kappa* are often used to approximate a hard G as in golf. *See pp24–5.*

Folk dancers perform at every festive occasion

THE ALPHABET AND VOCABULARY

Romanised spellings of Greek names can vary. More familiar Anglicised spellings (given in brackets in the headings) are sometimes used in the text. Other books and maps may use diferent spellings: *Nafplion, Navplion, Nauplion, Nafplio, Navplio* and *Nauplio* are all the same town. The differences are rarely so great as to make a name unrecognisable. The names of museums and other places of interest may also be translated differently, so that what one source interprets as 'Historical and Ethnological Museum' may be translated elsewhere as 'National Historical Museum'. To avoid confusion, placename headings give the name in romanised Greek, followed by the most usual English translation in brackets.

    It is helpful to know the Greek alphabet so that you can recognise placenames, while the few words and phrases following the alphabet will also come in handy.

PLACENAMES

Where a widely used English version of a placename exists, this is used throughout the text except in the initial placename heading. Such placenames include:

Athens (*Athínai*)

Corinth (*Kórinthos*)

Delphi (*Delfi*)

Epirus (*Ípiros*)

Kalamata (*Kalámai*)

Macedonia (*Makedhonia*)

Patras (*Pátrai*)

Sparta (*Spárti*)

Thebes (*Thivai*)

Thessaly (*Thessalía*)

Thrace (*Thráki*)

POSTAL ADDRESSES AND STREET NAMES

Odhos (street), *platia* (place or square) and *leoforos* (avenue) are usually dropped from Greek postal addresses. In this book, *odhos* and *leoforos* have accordingly been omitted but, in the interests of clarity, *platia* (as in Platia Sindagma) has been retained.

BASIC VOCABULARY

Yes	ne
No	ochi
Please/you're welcome	parakalo
Thank you	efkharisto
Excuse me	signomi
Hello	yasou
Goodbye	andio
Good morning	kalimera
Good evening	kalispera
Good night	kalanihta
Yesterday	htes
Today	simera
Tomorrow	avrio
How are you?	ti kanis
Do you speak English?	milate Anglika
I don't speak Greek	then milao Elinika
I don't understand	then katalaveno
Could you speak more slowly please?	parakalo, milate pio arga
Where is . . ?	Pou ine . . ?
How much is . . ?	poso kani . . ?
I would like . . .	tha ithela . . .

ALPHABET

Α, α	**alfa**	short *a*, as in hat
Β, β	**vita**	*v*, as in victory
Γ, γ	**ghamma**	*y*, as in you
Δ, δ	**Dhelta**	soft *th*, as in father
Ε, ε	**Epsilon**	short *e*, as in end
Ζ, ζ	**Zita**	*z*, as in zest
Η, η	**Ita**	long *e*, as in feet
Θ, θ	**Thita**	hard *th*, as in think
Ι, ι	**Yiota**	short *i*, as in hit
Κ, κ	**Kappa**	*k*, as in king
Λ, λ	**Lamdha**	*l*, as in loud
Μ, μ	**Mi**	*m*, as in mother
Ν, ν	**Ni**	*n*, as in no
Ξ, ξ	**Ksi**	*x*, as in box, or *ks*, as in books
Ο, ο	**Omikron**	*o*, as in orange
Π, π	**Pi**	*p*, as in peter
Σ, σ	**Sighma**	*s*, as in sing
Τ, τ	**Taf**	*t*, as in tea
Υ, υ	**Ipsilon**	long *e*, as in feet
Φ, φ	**Fi**	*f*, as in friend
Χ, χ	**Hi**	guttural *ch* sound, as in loch
Ψ, ψ	**Psi**	*ps*, as in lamps
Ω, ω	**Omegha**	*o*, as in orange

NUMBERS

1	ena	14	dhekatessera
2	dhio	15	dhekapende
3	tria	16	dhekaexi
4	tessera	17	dhekaevta
5	pende	18	dhekaokto
6	exi	19	dhekenea
7	evta	20	ikosi
8	okhto	30	trianda
9	enea	40	seranda
10	dheka	50	peninda
11	endheka	100	ekaton
12	dhodheka	1000	khilies
13	dhekatria		

Where to Go

Mainland Greece has more than enough sights and landscapes to fill any holiday and offers endless scope for exploration off the beaten track.

Ancient Greece

The ruins of ancient cities and temples clutter any map of Greece, but surprisingly few of the ancient sites which are so carefully marked and signposted are of interest to anyone except the keen archaeologist. They are, after all, up to 4,000 years old, and time has taken its toll. Even the best-preserved or most lovingly restored buildings lack roofs and many of the columns which supported them, while the statues and friezes which decorated them are either in museums or have been carted off by looters. The less well-preserved sites may be marked only by a single column, a scattering of masonry blocks, and a few holes in the ground. Of the scores of ancient sites carefully marked by the Greek Ministry of Culture, those of central Athens (*see pp34–7*) and a dozen or so others are guaranteed not to disappoint. These include the Temple of Poseidon at Soúnion (*see p46 & pp52–3*); Mikínai (Mycenae); Árgos and Tiryns in the Argolid; the nearby Theatre of Epídhavros (*see pp62–3*), and Corinth (*see p68*); Olympia in the western Peloponnese (*see p78*); and Delphi in the Sterea Ellás region (*see pp88–9*). Equally impressive are the remains of the temple complex at Dhodhóni in Epirus (*see p104*), and the sites of the lost cities of Dhion, below Mount Olympus (*see p128*), and Philippi (*see p120*).

In the southern Peloponnese, the mighty walls of ancient Ithomi are worth a detour.

Beaches

Mainland Greece offers excellent beaches, many of them surprisingly uncrowded. The longest and least developed sandy beaches run for many kilometres down the west coast of the Peloponnese, and in the southern Peloponnese there are also excellent sand beaches at Koróni, Methóni and Stoupa (*see pp64–5 & p76*). The more sheltered east coast of the Peloponnese boasts many delightful little beaches of white pebbles and coarse shingle.

In the north, there are excellent sand beaches on the Khalkidhikí (Chalkidiki) peninsulas (*see p122–3*), at Párga (*see p107*) on the west coast, and near Préveza (*see p107*).

Castles

Lovers of medieval romance should head for the Peloponnese, where it seems as though every hilltop and mountain pass is crowned by a Byzantine, Frankish or Turkish castle and every harbour has its Venetian fortress. Among the most striking are those at Mistra and Yeráki (*see pp74–5*), Monemvasía (*see pp72–3*), Koróni, Methóni and Pílos (*see pp64–5*) and Chlemoútsi (*see p78*).

Historic Towns

Towns with historic quarters which have survived the ravages of war, fire, earthquake and modernisation are easiest to find in the northern mainland. They include Ioánnina (*see p104*),

Kastoría (*see p128*), Kaválla, Komotiní and Xánthi (*see pp120–21*). In the south, Návplion (*see p61*) has a pretty town centre dating from its 18th-century Venetian heyday.

Mountains

The finest mountain scenery in Greece is to be found in the Pindhos range, which forms the backbone of the northern mainland. The Parnassós massif is an awesomely beautiful backdrop to Delphi, and the lonely peaks of Olympus dominate the plains of Thessaly and Macedonia. In the Peloponnese, the saw-edged ridge of the Taíyetos runs from the north to meet the sea at Ákra Taínaron (Cape Matapan), the southernmost tip of mainland Greece.

Picturesque Villages

Mainland villages display a rich variety of traditional architectural styles, from the ruined towers of the Mani (*see pp69–70 & pp80–81*) to the half-timbered mansions of the Pílion (Pelion) peninsula (*see pp112–13*), the stone-slab homes of the Zagória (*see pp114–15*) or the mud-brick ghost villages around the Préspa lakes (*see p128*).

Driving

Driving in Greece requires a combination of caution, confidence and strong nerves. Roads have been improved greatly in recent years and most are now well-surfaced but Greece is a mountainous country and there are many steep hairpin bends. Greek bus drivers, who like to take these hairpins at speed, usually sound their horns almost continuously to tell you that they are coming. Among other typically Greek hazards are flocks of goats or sheep being herded across the main road, usually when you least expect them.

In places, wide, newly tarred roads degenerate abruptly and without warning into pot-holed tracks, a spine-jarring experience for driver and passengers. Greek drivers will take an ordinary saloon car over the roughest roads, but off the beaten track some roads are suitable only for four-wheel-drive vehicles.

Outside the three major cities and the main highways which connect them traffic is light. In the cities, it is another story: driving, navigating and finding somewhere to park can be demanding, and it is easier to leave your car and explore on foot or by public transport.

There are one-way systems in even the smallest villages. These are widely ignored by locals.

Greeks are aggressive drivers, and a combination of winding roads and cavalier driving habits results in the worst road accident level in Europe, with almost 2,000 fatalities a year. Speed limits are treated with contempt (Greek drivers flash their lights at oncoming traffic to warn of police checkpoints) and though seat belts are compulsory for drivers and front-seat passengers, not all Greeks abide by this law.

If all this sounds intimidating, do not let it deter you from driving in Greece. Driving can be by far the best way to see the country, and a car will take you to places impossible to reach by public transport. The golden rule for drivers in Greece is: expect the unexpected.

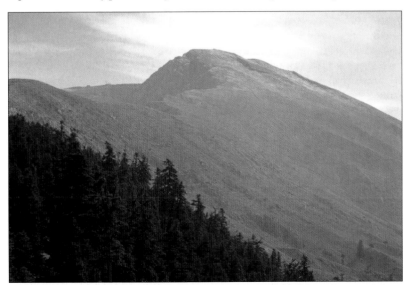

The slopes of the Parnassós massif, backdrop for the beauties of ancient Delphi

Athínai

Athens

Athens is home to almost 30 per cent of the country's total population, and the glowing columns of the Parthenon, the city's best-loved landmark, rise above the crag of the Acropolis like an island of grace in a modern urban sea.

Much of Athens is surprisingly new, built since World War II to house an influx of people from the countryside. In 1940 only 850,000 people lived in the city. By 1970, there were 2.5 million. Today there are 3.2 million.

The city's apartment and office blocks nevertheless conceal happy surprises. Turn any corner and you may find yourself looking at a 1,000-year-old church, a tiny park cluttered with toppled ancient columns, a quaint old *tavérna* or the high garden wall of a 19th-century mansion surrounded by exotic palm trees.

Athens has only one major city-centre park, Ethnikós Kípos (National Gardens), but makes up for its shortage of public green space with explosions of greenery and colour from gardens, balconies and window-boxes. Plants and orange trees line streets and squares, jasmine and honeysuckle cling to tumbledown walls and in spring even wasteland and roadside blaze briefly with wild poppies and daisies.

City life echoes the laid-back style of a rural village, and few corners are without a vendor peddling a variety of

tit-bits to nibble on such as barbecued corn-cobs, nuts, sunflower seeds, or sesame-seed rings.

As is common practice in Mediterranean cities, most offices close for an

Central Athens

afternoon siesta, and Athenians spend much of their leisure time playing backgammon or (as befits folk who live in the city where democracy was born) arguing politics at café tables.

Most of the city's ancient sites and museums are in a compact area within a two-kilometer radius of Platia Sindagma (Constitution Square), the hub of modern Athens.

Akrópolis

Acropolis

Time and weather have stripped the buildings of the Acropolis to bare white marble, making the perfect simplicity of their proportions all the more striking. Their impact reaches across more than two millennia.

The restored Temple of Athena Nike

The 100-m limestone crag was first occupied more than 5,000 years ago, and there are traces of Mycenaean buildings dating from 1500 BC. In the 5th century BC Pericles – the city's leading statesman and its guiding hand from 461 to 430 BC – commissioned Kallikrates and Iktinos (both after 450 BC) to rebuild the temples sacked by the Persians in 480 BC, and the brilliant Phidias (500–432 BC) to design their friezes and statues.

Later occupiers demolished some buildings. Others (including the Parthenon) were damaged or destroyed during the many sieges of the Acropolis between medieval and modern times. As late as the War of Independence, Greek rebels used it as a fortress.

The main buildings of the site are linked by the Sacred Way, running from the middle gate of the Propylaia to the Parthenon. The site is entered by the eastern Beulé Gate, to the left of which stands the plinth of a statue to the Roman general Agrippa.
Tel: (210) 321 0219. Open: daily, summer 8am–7pm; winter 8.30am–3pm. Admission charge (includes entry to museum and Acropolis site).

Eréchtheion

Restored in the 1980s, the Eréchtheion was the Acropolis's holiest shrine, dedicated to Athena as patroness of Athens. Standing opposite the Parthenon, its three Ionic porticos were built on different levels. The original caryatids (female figures) of the south portico have been replaced by copies.

Mousío Akrópoli (Acropolis Museum)

Exhibits include figures of Athena, 6th-century BC *korae* (figures of draped maidens), friezes from the Eréchtheion and the Temple of Athena Nike, and caryatids from the Eréchtheion.
Tel: (210) 323 6665. Open: as the Acropolis.

Naós Athená Níke (Temple of Athena Nike)

The temple honours Athena as goddess of victory. Designed by Kallikrates in the mid-5th century BC to celebrate the Athenian defeat of Persia, it was completed in 424 BC. Demolished by the Turks, it was restored in the 19th century.

Parthenón

Phidias and his patron Pericles intended the Parthenon to be an act of worship in stone, celebrating Athens at the zenith of its power.

Dedicated to Athena in 438 BC, the Parthenon was brightly painted and cluttered with elaborately decorated statues. The greatest, the gold and ivory statue of Athena, 12m high, was taken to Constantinople in AD 426 and melted down. A copy is in the National Archaeological Museum (*see p40*).

In the Middle Ages the Parthenon was used as a Christian church, and in 1466 it became a Turkish mosque. The Turks later used it as a powder magazine.

Propylaea (Propylaia)

The Propylaia, the dramatic gateway to the Acropolis temple complex, combined Ionic and Doric features. Built between 437 and 432 BC by the architect Mnesikles, its 46-m wide portico was pierced by five elaborate gates. The north wing of the Propylaia housed the Pinakotheke, which was built in the 5th century BC as a portrait gallery. The Pinakotheke was in use as a powder magazine when it was struck by lightning in 1645. It has been partly restored.

The Sacred Way

After entering the temple site by the Propylaia, worshippers passed along the flag-stoned Sacred Way, lined with statues of deities and heroes, to the Parthenon, pausing to worship at one or all of the shrines on the way. There are fine views of Athens from here.

The Parthenon Marbles

In the early 19th century, when Greece was under Turkish domination, Lord Elgin, British ambassador to the Ottoman Sultan, obtained permission from the authorities to " . . . take away some pieces of stone with old inscriptions or figures there on . . . ."

The 'pieces of stone' he carried away were marble friezes which adorned the Parthenon and Temple of Athena Nike, removed in 1801 at the cost of terrible damage to the temple edifice. These are now housed in the British Museum in London. Greeks strongly resent this and their demand that the marbles be returned is supported by many archaeologists and and historians the world over.

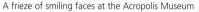

A frieze of smiling faces at the Acropolis Museum

The temples of ancient Greece still have the power to move the visitor after two and a half millennia – an amazing tribute to their builders. The architects of classical Greece picked the setting for each temple as carefully as they planned its proportions. Besotted with the possibilities of geometry, they strove for simplicity, harmony and balance through a complex series of interrelated ratios. Few designers in the intervening centuries have matched their talents.

The temples of the 6th and 5th centuries BC, the golden age of Greek architecture, were built to a strict pattern. Steps surrounded a rectangular stone platform which supported fluted columns topped by a gabled roof and decorated with elaborate friezes depicting gods, heroes and monsters. Again and again, the builders managed the brilliant trick of making the massive marble columns seem light and delicate, balancing height against width and horizontal against vertical by the use of the simplest of harmonic ratios.

Doric temple architecture, originating in mainland Greece, was the earliest and plainest of the three 'orders' of classical architecture. Columns had no base, a simple capital at the top, and no more than 20 flutes or decorative grooves. Doric temples, like the superbly preserved Temple of Apollo at Vassai, can appear more massive than those built in the Ionian style. The Parthenon, finest of all the Doric buildings, avoids this by sleight of hand: its columns slope slightly inward for strength, and the corner columns, which should appear larger than the others, are in fact slightly smaller, tricking the eye into seeing a larger space. The Ionic style originated among the Greek cities of the Asia Minor coast. Ionic columns have a subdivided base, a shaft with 20 flutes, a decorated capital, and are often slimmer than the Doric column. The later Corinthian style, developed after the Roman conquest of Greece, is a fusion of Greek and Roman design. Base and shaft are similar to Ionic columns, while the cup-shaped capital is more floridly carved with leaves and garlands.

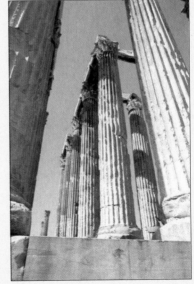

Facing page: caryatids of the Eréchtheion
Above: the Parthenon; right: Corinthian
columns of the Olympion Dhios

AROUND THE ACROPOLIS
New Acropolis Museum
Although originally scheduled for 2004 as the new home for the controversial Elgin Marbles currently housed in the British Museum, this modern all-glass museum looks unlikely to open before 2007.
Acropolis Hill.

Lófos Filopápou (Hill of the Muses)
Named after the Roman consul Philopappos, the hill is topped by his 12-m high monumental tomb, built in AD 116. Around it are the remnants of 3rd-century BC fortifications.

Odíon Iródou Attikó (Odeon of Herod Atticus)
Built into the rock of the Acropolis in AD 161, this huge theatre is the main venue for the annual Athens Festival of music, theatre and dance. It seats 6,000, and its superb acoustics carry voices to the highest of its many tiers of seats.

The theatre's well-preserved Roman façade with its tiers of arches can be viewed from the stepped path to the Acropolis, which runs past it.
Dhionissou Areopayitou.
Open: for performances only (see p149).

Olympíon Dhiós and Píli Adhrianoú (Olympian Zeus and Arch Of Hadrian)
The temple of Olympian Zeus was one of the ancient world's greatest, completed by the Roman Emperor Hadrian in AD 132. It measured 107.5m by 41m. Only 15 of its 84 columns still stand, the rest having been taken by successive occupiers of Athens,

Tiers of seats ring the auditorium of the Theatre of Dionysos

including Genoese, Venetians and Turks, for building stone.

Next to the Temple of Olympian Zeus, the monumental arch divided Hadrian's new Roman city from older Hellenic Athens.
Junction of Leoforos Singrou and Leoforos Amalias. Tel: (210) 922 6330.
Open: daily, summer 8am–7pm; winter 8.30am–3pm. Admission charge.

Pnyx
On this low hill west of the Acropolis the Athenian popular assembly met until the late 4th century BC, when it relocated to the Théatro Dhionissou (Theatre of Dionysos) below the Acropolis.

Théatro Dhioníssou (Theatre of Dionysos)
The oldest of the buildings on the southern slope of the Acropolis, the 17,000-seat theatre with its 67 tiers of seats is separated from the Odeon of Herod Atticus by the sites of the

Sanctuaries of Asklepios and of Dionysos Eleutheros, of which only two Corinthian columns remain. Built in the 4th century BC, the theatre was embellished and enlarged in the 1st century AD under the Roman emperor Nero, with the addition of elaborately carved front-row seats for the priests of Dionysos and other dignitaries.

Next to the theatre are the remains of two sanctuaries to Asklepios, god of healing, dating from the 4th and 5th centuries BC, and the rows of column bases which mark the site of the 2nd-century BC Stoa of Eumenes.

Dhionissou Areopayitou.
Tel: (210) 322 4625.
Open: as the Acropolis.

NORTH OF THE ACROPOLIS
Agorá (Ancient Market-place)

This was the heart of everyday life in ancient Athens and after the Acropolis is the most important and evocative of the city's ancient sites. Highlights include the 5th-century BC Thission, the most intact of all Greece's temples. So called because its friezes (now badly damaged) showed the exploits of Theseus, the building with its 34 Doric columns was a temple to Ifestos (Hephaestos), the armourer of the gods and the deity of smiths and artisans.

Rebuilt after the Persian invasion of 480 BC, the Agorá was ringed by long, colonnaded buildings called *stoas*. One of these, the 2nd-century BC Stoa

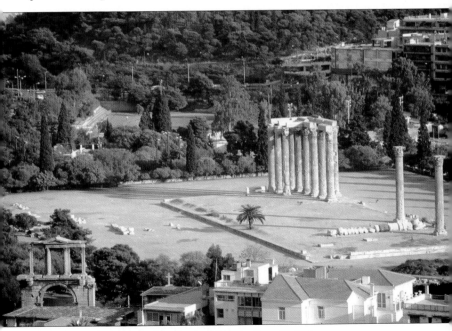

Only 15 of the original columns of the Temple of Olympian Zeus still stand

Attalou (Stoa of Attalos II), was rebuilt by American archaeologists. A striking two-storey building with a Doric colonnade on the ground floor and an Ionic one above, it is now the Mousío Agorá (Agorá Museum), with a collection of vases and fragmented statues. Just below the upper entrance to the site stands the Byzantine church of Áyioi Apostoloi, built in the 11th century AD on a site on which St Paul is said to have preached.
Main entrance is on Adhrianoú., 5 minutes walk from Monastiráki metro station. Tel: (210) 321 0185. Open: daily, summer 8am–7pm; winter 8.30am–3pm. Admission charge.

Ários Págos (Areopagus)

According to legend it was on this rocky hilltop above the site of the ancient Agorá that Ares the war god was tried by the other Olympians for the murder of one of the sons of Poseidon. A cave in the hillside was the Sanctuary of the Eumenides (the Harpies), who were goddesses of revenge. The summit offers views of the Ancient Agorá and the Acropolis.

Keramikós Cemetery and Museío

The cemetery of ancient Athens was excavated in the 19th century, revealing rows of *stelae* (tombstones) of the Athenian élite. Others are on show in the small museum and in the National Archaeological Museum (*see p40*).
Ermou 148. Tel: (210) 346 3552. Open: daily, summer 8am–7pm; winter 8.30am–3pm. Admission charge.

Náos Eólou (Tower of the Winds)

Overlooking the Roman Forum, this 13-m high octagonal marble building was built in the 1st century AD. The tower takes its name from the winged figures carved on each face to represent the winds, and housed a water-clock for those using the nearby Forum.
Near junction of Eólou and Adhrianoú, opposite Romaiki Agorá. Not open to the public.

Romaikí Agorá (Roman Forum)

The site of the Roman market-place, which complemented the nearby Ancient Agorá, is marked by the massive four-

The tombstone of an Athenian noble family in the Keramikos cemetery columned gateway built in the 2nd century AD. There is little else to see within the site.

Pelopida and Eólou. Tel: (210) 324 5220. Open: daily 8am–5pm. Admission charge.

MODERN ATHENS

The main thoroughfares, squares and public buildings of modern Athens date from the 19th century, when Otho I, first king of independent Greece, decreed a new capital among the ancient ruins. Sadly, much of Otho's gracious little capital was destroyed during World War II, and post-war development has swamped the rest.

Ethnikós Kípos (National Gardens)

Laid out for Otho I's queen, Amalia, by a Bavarian landscape architect, the former garden of the Anáktora (Royal Palace, now the Voulí, the Parliament

The ancient Agorá in Athens, once the social and commercial hub of the city

The Tower of the Winds and columns of the Roman market-place

Building) is the only large green space in central Athens. A band plays at its open-air café on summer evenings.
The entrance gates are on Amalias, Iródou and Vasilissis Sofias. Open: sunrise–sunset. Free admission.

Kolonáki

The smartest shops, nightspots and restaurants in Athens are in this fashionable suburb on the slopes of Likavitós, 10 minutes' walk from Sindagma. The centre of Kolonaki is Platia Kolonaki, a central square ringed by chic cafés and piano bars. Behind it, steep streets and steps climb the hill.

Likavitós

This wooded 22-m high peak, topped by the chapel of Áyios Yioryios (St George), is a prominent landmark, from which there are fine views of the Acropolis, the city and its surroundings. A path leads to the chapel from the Hotel St George-Lykabettos, Kleomenous 2. The lazy way is to take the funicular, also from Kleomenous.

Mitropólis (Cathedral)

The massive and ugly new cathedral, built in the 19th century, dwarfs the much prettier late 12th-century building next to it, uniquely built of fragments from ancient temples and medieval buildings. Many of the ancient fragments have had crosses carved on them later.
Platia Mitropólis.

Omónia

Platia Omonia, at the opposite end of Stadhiou from Sindagma, is the city's other main square. Once elegant, it has

The whitewashed chapel of Áyios Yioryios on Likavitós

become a busy traffic and public transport hub with little of its former charm.

Piraiévs (Piraeus)

The port of Athens, west of the city, is connected to it by a single metro line. You will have to pass through the harbour district to visit the islands of the Argolikós-Saronikós Kólpos (Argo-Saronic Gulf), though many of the excursion boats now leave from Faliron Bay to the west of Piraeus (*see pp134–5*).

Mikrolímano (Little Harbour)

Sometimes called Turkolimano (Turkish Harbour), Mikrolimano is between Piraeus itself and Faliron. This lagoon-like one-time fishing harbour is now filled with yachts but is still surrounded by the best fish restaurants in Athens, almost two dozen of them.

Pláka

Below the Acropolis, on its north and east sides, the old-fashioned streets of the Plaka with their tall, stucco-fronted houses and occasional gardens full of palms or lemon trees are the prettiest part of Athens. There are few cars and plenty of shops, cafés, restaurants and leafy squares. Tourism plays a big role, but has not yet taken over the Plaka completely. The main shopping street is Adhrianoú, running around the northwest edge of the Plaka.

Síndagma

Platia Sindagma is the heart of modern Athens, surrounded by expensive hotels, banks and airline offices, and open-air cafés. The meeting-point of the city's main avenues – Ermou, Amalias, Stadhiou and Venizelou (also called Panepisthimiou) – Sindagma is an island in a sea of traffic. The drills and diggers at work on the new Athens underground system (scheduled for completion by the end of the century) somewhat detract from its undoubted appeal.

Stádion (Stadium)

This copy in marble of the ancient Stadium, built in stone in 330 BC and rebuilt in marble in AD 140, dates from the late 19th century. It was donated to the Greek people by the millionaire George Averof in time for the first modern Olympic Games in 1896.
Junction of Vasileos Konstandinou and Iródou Attikou. Open for events only.

Voulí (Parliament)

Borrowing the name of the ancient Athenian citizens' council, the Voulí is the most imposing of the city's 19th-century buildings. Built in 1843 as the palace of Otho I, the building and the Tomb of the Unknown Soldier outside it are guarded by white-kilted élite soldiers of the Evzones regiment.
Leoforos Amalias, east side of Syntagma. Not open to the public. Changing of the Guard, 11am on Sun.

Brightly painted houses like this 19th-century mansion are typical of the old Plaka

Záppion

This elegant cream-and-yellow building standing in formal gardens is the epitome of the neo-classical style popular in the reign of Otho I. Its most noteworthy feature is its mock-Corinthian portico. Completed in 1883, it was the gift to the city of millionaire Constantine Zappas, and is now a conference centre.
Located within the National Gardens. Open: sunrise–sunset.

MUSEUMS OF ATHENS
Ethnikí Pinakothíki
(National Art Gallery)

Three paintings by El Greco (born in Venetian-ruled Crete though he worked in Spain) are the jewels of the gallery's collection. Most of its other paintings are by 19th-century Romantics.
Vasileos Konstandinou 50. Tel: (210) 821 7717. Open: Mon–Sat 9am–3pm, Sun 10am–2pm. Admission charge.

Istorikó Mousío
(National Historical Museum)

This contains an exhibition of paintings, engravings, weapons and relics devoted to the Greek struggle for independence from the Middle Ages to the 20th century.
Stadhiou 13. Tel: (210) 323 7617. Open: Tue–Fri 9am–1.30pm, Sat & Sun 9am–12.30pm. Admission charge.

Mousío Arkheologikó Ethnikó
(National Archaeological Museum)

Whatever you do in Athens, do not miss the finest museum in Greece, scheduled to reopen in April 2004, following extensive refurbishment. Objects on display include treasures from the royal tombs of Mycenae (notably the dazzling gold 'Mask of Agamemnon'), classical frescoes from Thira (on the island of Santorini), a magnificent 5th century BC bronze statue of Poseidon, richly decorated black-and-red figure vases from the 6th and 5th century BC, plus the newly opened Egyptian Wing. It is well worth devoting most of a day to the huge collection. If you try to rush round, you will miss some of the most striking highlights.
Patission 44. Tel: (210) 821 7717. Open: summer, Mon 12.30pm–7pm, Tue–Fri 8am–7pm, Sat & Sun 8.30am–3pm; winter, Mon 11 am–5pm, Tue–Fri 8am–5pm, Sat & Sun 8.30am–3pm. Admission charge.

Mousío Athinón
(Athens Museum)

For a glimpse of Athens during its 19th-century revival, visit the former royal palace, where a collection of paintings and exhibits is housed in one of the prettiest of the city's surviving neo-classical buildings.
Paparigopoulou 7. Tel: (210) 324 6164. Open: Mon, Wed, Fri & Sat, 9am–1.30pm. Admission charge.

Mousío Benáki
(Benaki Museum)

Reopened in 2000 following total renovation, this fascinating museum traces Greek art and handcrafts from the Stone Age right up to the formation of the modern Greek state (1834). Objects are displayed in chronological order: look out for Bronze Age metalwork, Byzantine jewellery and icons, paintings by El Greco and a reconstruction of a

wood-panelled reception room from an 18th-century mansion. There's also an excellent café on the top floor.
Konmbari 1, Kolanaki. Tel: (210) 367 1000; www.benaki.gr
Open: Mon, Wed, Fri & Sat, 9am-5pm, Thu 9am-midnight, Sun 9am-3pm. Admission charge.

Mousío Elliníkis Laografías (Museum of Greek Folk Art)
Here you will find an eye-catching collection of delicate embroideries and magnificent clerical robes, and also traditional pottery from the islands.
Kidhathíneon 17. Tel: (210) 321 3018. Open: Tue–Sun 10am–2pm. Admission charge.

Mousío Ellinikon Mousikon Organon (Museum of Greek Musical Instruments)
Housed in a neo-classical mansion in the heart of Plaka, this charming museum contains a stunning collection of traditional Greek musical instruments. Each display case is accompanied by a headset, so you can listen to the instruments being played, and a video at the entrance shows how the individual instruments are made.
Diogenous 1–3. Tel: (210) 325 0198. Open: Tue & Thu–Sun 10am–2pm, Wed noon–6pm. Free admission.

Mousío Goulandrí Kikládhikí Téxni (Goulandris Museum of Cycladic and Ancient Greek Art)
More than 200 startlingly modern-looking statuettes, tools, weapons and ceramics from the Cycladic civilisation which dominated Greece between 3000 and 2000 BC are displayed here.
Neofytou Douka 4. Tel: (210) 722 8321. Open: Mon–Wed & Fri 10am–4pm, Sat 10am–1pm. Admission charge.

Polemikó Mousío (War Museum)
Housed in an ugly 1960s block, this museum was created by the Colonels' junta to glorify the army. It offers an insight into Greece's deep vein of patriotism, fostered by struggles against so many invaders, but the antique aircraft which sit outside and the collections of obsolete weapons and battle tableaux within are not very exciting.
Vasilissis Sofias 24 and Rizari. Tel: (210) 729 0543. Open: Tue–Sun 9am–2pm. Free admission.

Vizandinó Mousío (Byzantine Museum)
Icons are the chief glory of this collection, though the best-known exhibit is the Epitaphios of Thessaloníki, a 14th-century embroidery depicting the Lamentation.
Vasilissis Sofias 22. Tel: (210) 723 1570. Open: Tue–Sun 8.30am–3pm. Admission charge.

The Goulandris Museum

Walk: The Plaka and the Acropolis

The Plaka is the most picturesque part of Athens and alone of the older districts has survived fairly intact. Its narrow streets offer an escape from the manic Athens traffic.
Allow up to 4 hours.

Start at Monastiráki metro station and head down Ifaistou (Ifestou) into the Flea Market, a mix of jewellers, souvenir shops, shoemakers, boutiques and army surplus stores.

1 Platía Avissinías

About five minutes' walk from Monastiráki, turn away from the boutiques and souvenir shops of Ifaistou

for a look at an old-fashioned clutter of furniture-makers, antique stalls and street vendors selling junk of all kinds. *At the end of Ifaistou turn left then left again on to Adhrianou.*

2 Ancient Agorá

Entering the Agorá by its lower gate, follow the signs to the Thission for one of the best views in Athens. Most of the modern city is hidden. Mount Imittós dominates the eastern skyline with the wooded slopes of Ários Págos to the south, and above them the crag of the Acropolis and the pillars of the Parthenon. As a bonus, the whole of the Agorá, the heart of the ancient city, is laid out in front of you (*see p35*).

3 Áyioi Apóstoloi

Before leaving the Agorá by the upper gate, pause to look at the domed Áyioi Apostoloi (Holy Apostles), a Byzantine church dating from the 11th century and built on a site where St Paul is said to have preached.
Leaving the Agorá, turn left and left again, and then right on to Polignotou.

4 Romaikí Agorá
(The Roman Agorá/Forum)

A four-columned portico marks the entrance to the site of the Roman Agorá. To the north stands the site of the Vivliothiki Adhrianoú (currently closed for excavation). On the east side of the site stands Náos Eólou (Tower of the Winds). Built in the 1st century BC, it was a combined sundial and water-clock.
Turn right on Dioskouron, a steep street of old-fashioned, yellow-painted stucco houses which becomes a flight of steps before it joins Theorias. Theorias runs above the Ancient Agorá, passes between the Acropolis and the Ários Págos and curves left to the entrance to the Acropolis (see pp30–31).
The uphill part of the walk ends here. From the Acropolis take the stepped path downhill through pine trees for about 100m and turn left.

5 Odíon Iródou Attikó
(Odeon of Herod Atticus)

This fine Roman theatre was built in AD 161. Athens Festival events are staged here in summer. It is open only for performances (*see p34*).
Descend a short flight of steps to emerge on to busy Dhionissou Areopayitou. Turn left and walk downhill for 200m past the Theatre of Dionysus.

6 Théatro Dhioníssou
(Theatre of Dionysos)

The works of the great Athenian playwrights were first performed in this theatre, which dates from about 534 BC (*see pp34–5*).
At the foot of Dhionissou Areopayitou, turn left on to Vironos and follow it to Platia Lisikrati.

7 Platía Lisikráti

Marked by the 4th-century BC Lysikrates Monument, whose six Corinthian half-columns commemorate a prizewinning *choregos* (choirmaster), this is a good place to stop for a drink or a meal.
Vironos leads on to Selley. At its end, turn right then immediately left, back on to Adhrianoú.

8 Shopping on Adhrianoú and Pandrósou

Adhrianoú is lined with shops selling clothes and a range of traditional crafts including pottery and brightly coloured rugs and carpets.
Turn right on to Eólou, then left on to Pandrosou. This 'new' flea-market street with its dozens of souvenir shops leads back to Monastiráki.

Attikí

Attica

Attica is the mythic heartland of ancient Greece and it takes only a little while to escape from Athens to the little-changed landscape of the Messogia, in the midst of the southern peninsula. Covered with vineyards and olive groves as it has been since antiquity, the region produces much of the *retsina* drunk in Athenian *tavérnas*.

The Temple of Themis (goddess of Justice) at Rhamnoós, destroyed by the Persians

On the southern tip of the peninsula, the columns of the Temple of Poseidon, dramatically silhouetted against the sunset, are one of the great sights. Other delightful temples are to be seen at Vravróna and Thorikón (Thorikos), on the peninsula's east coast.

A string of fashionably casual seaside suburbs, beaches and marinas on the west coast of the Attica peninsula attracts droves of Athenians in summer. The best sandy beaches, though, are on the bay of Marathón, 42km from Athens, where a mound and a modern monument mark the grave of the Athenians who fell in battle against the Persians in 490 BC. Northwest of Athens, grim fortresses and ghostly battlefields mark the one-time frontier of Athens with Thebes, its rival. The fortresses of Aigósthena, Elevtherai and Plataiaí mark where the Spartans, Athenians and their allies again defeated the Persians in 479.

West of Athens, the coastal highway to Corinth passes through industrial suburbs which generate much of the capital's notorious smog.

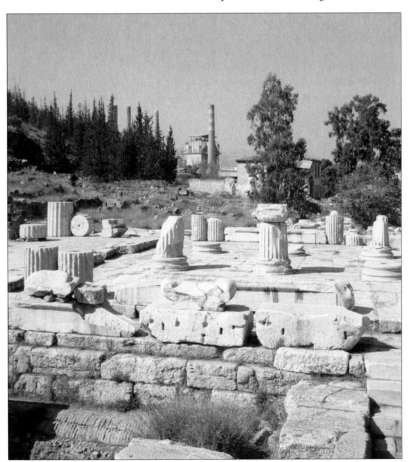

The ruins of Eleusis (see p50), once one of the most important religious shrines in Greece

THE PLAYGROUND OF ATHENS: AKTÍ APÓLLONA (APOLLO COAST)

South of Athens lie the city's seaside suburbs and marinas, offering Athenians a summer getaway. Pollution is a problem on beaches closer to the busy harbour of Piraiévs (Piraeus), and swimming between Piraeus and Glifádha is not recommended. Beyond this, a string of clean beaches extends along the west-facing Aktí Apollona (Apollo Coast) to the tip of the peninsula.

Akrá Soúnion (Cape Soúnion)

After the Acropolis, the **Temple of Poseidon** in silhouette against the sunset is the best-known and most striking image of Attica. Perched 60m above the sea on the peninsula's southern tip, the temple, dedicated to Poseidon, was built between 444 and 440 BC. It was restored after independence in the 19th century with 16 Doric columns of the original 34 surviving. Just 6.10m high, the columns seem taller because of their slimness, measuring only 1m in diameter at the base and

0.8m at the top. On one of the two columns of the entrance portico is carved the name of Lord Byron, who visited the temple in 1810.

The temple is at its most spectacular at sunset, when it is also at its most crowded as dozens of sightseeing coaches arrive from Athens.
Temple of Poseidon, 70km south of Athens. Tel: (229) 203 9363. Open: daily 10am–sunset. Admission charge.

Glifádha (Glyfadha)

The best swimming near Athens is at Glyfadha , the smart suburb 18km from the city centre, favoured by wealthy Athenians and expatriates. There is a clean beach operated by the National Tourist Organisation, a marina and the capital's only 18-hole golf course (*see p158*).

Koutoúki Cave

The Koutoúki Cave, discovered in 1926, plunges into the side of Imittós. Within, water trickles down floodlit rose-coloured walls and needle-sharp stalactites.
4km from the village of Paianía (Peania) and 18km from Athens.

ANCIENT ATTICA

Theseus, the mythical king who slew the Minotaur, and thus freed Athens from paying tribute to the Minoan rulers of Knossos, united the petty kingdoms of Attica with Athens. Throughout ancient times the region remained part of the Athenian city-state, providing Athens with wine, bread, olives, marble for its great temples and silver from the Lavrion mines. During the Peloponnesian War of the 5th century BC, Sparta struck at Athens by invading Attica each year, systematically felling its olive groves and cutting off the city's food supply.

With the decline of Athens, Attica declined too and as Christianity took over, its temples fell into disuse, to be rediscovered only in the 19th century.

*Tel: (210) 664 2910. Open: daily
9am–4.30pm. Admission charge.*

Vári

Vari comes to bubbling life after dark,
when it is a favourite dinner destination
for Athenians. Waiters dressed in
traditional baggy pants and embroidered waistcoats drum up business for
dozens of rival restaurants. Not for
vegetarians or the faint-hearted, Vari's
taverns cater to serious carnivores with
dishes like whole lamb on the spit,
skewered meat, *kokoretsi* (spit-roasted
lamb entrails) and sheep's brains.
27km from Athens.

Várkiza

A lively resort and fishing harbour,
Várkiza has a 750m stretch of sand with
facilities operated by the National
Tourist Organisation. Cafés and
expensive restaurants surround its small
port and many Athenians drive out for
the evening, especially at weekends, to
sample freshly caught seafood.
31km south of Athens.

Vouliagméni

The smartest of all the resort suburbs,
Vouliagméni is the haunt of Athenian
shipping millionaires and other tycoons,
as can be seen from the luxury yachts
and cruisers at anchor in its marina.
Villas and hotels are dotted among the
pine trees of two wooded headlands
framing Vouliagméni's natural harbour.
Vouliagméni's beaches and luxury hotels
are popular and crowded in summer.
24km south of Athens.

The richly stocked yacht marina in the fashionable Athenian suburb of Glyfadha

MARATHÓN AND THE EAST COAST
Amfiaraíon

Located in a peaceful, pine-covered gully, rows of stone coffins and statue pedestals give a clear picture of the layout of the ancient site, a sanctuary dedicated to the legendary Amphiaraos, king of Argos, and dating from the 4th century BC. The lion-footed seats of the priests in the front row of its 3,000-seat theatre are well preserved.

On the Kálamos road, 38km north of Athens. Tel: (229) 506 2144. Open: Tue–Sun 8.30am–2.30pm. Admission charge.

Marathón

The name is legendary but there is little to see at Marathón. The only relic of the battle is the 12-m high mound marking the tomb of the 192 Athenians who fell. It stands among citrus groves behind a 2km crescent of sandy beach.

The mound of the Plataians, allies of Athens, is 5km away on the opposite (inland) side of the main road near the small village of **Vranas**. Next to it, the Marathón Archaeological Museum houses finds from the tomb, gravestones and carvings from the mid-4th century BC, pottery and stone tools from the Cycladic and Mycenaean eras, and an Egyptian-style *kouros* from the 2nd century BC. In the adjacent Bronze Age tomb, 10 skeletons dating from the 2nd millennium BC are open to view.

Tomb and museum: 42km from Athens and 5km from

Temple of Artemis, Vravróna. Beyond the foundations are the dining rooms and dormitories of the young priestesses that served here

THE BATTLE OF MARATHON

With its long sweep of gently shelving beach, the bay of Mara-thónas is the perfect place for a seaborne invasion, and it was here in 490 BC that the Persian general Mardonios landed with a fleet and an army of perhaps 30,000. They were met by 10,000 Athenians and their Plataian allies. Though heavily outnumbered, the Athenians charged the Persians and routed them. The Athenian historians claimed only 192 of their citizen soldiers were killed (among them the Athenian commander Kallimakhos) for 6,400 Persian dead. Miltiades, the surviving commander, sent a runner to tell the city of the victory. He ran non-stop, gasping out his news before dying of exhaustion and inspiring the modern marathon event, run over a course which corresponds to the distance from the battlefield to the city of Athens.

*the resort of Marathón. Tel: (229) 405
5155. Open: Tue–Sun 8.30am–3pm.
Admission charge.*

Rafína

Ferries and hydrofoils to the Aegean
islands lend an air of bustle to this small
port. Its half-moon harbour front is
packed with excellent fish *tavérnas*, a
lovely place for a night out. In the
daytime, Evia and the slopes of Oxi
Oros tantalise on the horizon.
40km east of Athens.

Rhamnoós (Ramnous)

Ramnous is now off the beaten track,
but in ancient times it controlled all the
shipping passing through the Gulf of
Evia. The most impressive part of the
site, the 4th-century BC fortified
harbour, is closed for further archaeological work. The site is famous for its
Temple of Nemesis, the goddess of
justice, retribution and atonement, built
about 435 BC, which is the only such
temple known outside Asia Minor, and
the Temple of Themis, the goddess of
world order, built about 500 BC.
*Káto Soúli, 55km northeast of Athens,
follow signs from main Marathón road.
Tel: (229) 406 3477. Open: daily
8.30am–2.30pm. Admission charge.*

Thorikón (Thorikos)

A short distance from the ugly mining
town of Lávrion, close to Attica's
southern tip, ancient Thorikos is still
being excavated. Quite densely populated
from 2900 BC onwards, the town became
a Mycenaean stronghold, and three
16th-century BC beehive graves have
been discovered. Its most interesting

The burial mound at Marathón, beneath which
archaeologists found bones of the Athenian dead

feature is an unusual 4th-century BC
oval-shaped theatre with tiers of seats
for 5,000 spectators.
*Signposted 'Theatre Antique' from
Lávrion. Free admission.*

Vravróna (Brauron)

Here you will find a cluster of graceful
temple columns among vineyards and
reedbeds. The earliest finds from the site
are from as early as 1700 BC, but the main
ruins are those of the 5th-century BC
Temple of Artemis, the goddess of female
chastity, a cult which goes back to the
9th century BC, possibly founded by
Iphigenia, daughter of Agamemnon. A
small museum exhibits jewellery and
sacred vessels from the temple. More
interesting are the lively statues of the
arktoi or 'bear-maidens' who were the
priestesses of Artemis. The 15th century
AD chapel of Áyios Yioryios, within the
temple precinct, has some interesting
remains of frescoes.
*Vravróna Archaeological Site, signposted
on the road to Pórto Ráfti, 7km from
Markópoulon. Tel: (229) 202 7020.
Open: Tue–Sun 8.30am–3pm.
Admission charge.*

NORTHERN ATTIKA
Dafní Monastery

The monastery and church of the Virgin at Dafní date from the 11th century AD, though there has been a monastery on the site since the 6th century. Much of the splendid gold mosaic of the interior survives; its most striking feature is the mosaic of a characteristically stern-looking, Byzantine-style Christ, though the other portraits are very human, lively and almost classical in their rendering. The exterior, with its graceful arcade and portico, using columns and fragments lifted from an earlier temple of Apollo, is less stolid than many modern Orthodox churches and is a typical Byzantine mix of brickwork and masonry. *Signposted off the main Athens-Eleusís-Corinth highway, 11km from the centre of Athens. Tel: (210) 5811 558. Open: daily 8.30am–3pm. Admission charge.*

Elevsís (Eleusis)

Set on a low hill overlooking the sea and surrounded by refineries and factories, Eleusis is now an unprepossessing place but it was one of the great sanctuaries of ancient times. Dedicated to the fertility goddesses Persephone and Demeter, the site was rediscovered and excavated in the 19th century. Roman ruins overlay the earlier Greek

Thebes Archaeological Museum

temple. Its main features are the great forecourt and entrance to the sanctuary built by the Romans in the 2nd century AD, the Telesterion, which was the centre of the sanctuary, and the classical-era defensive walls around the site.
Eleusís Archaeological Site, signposted from the main Athens-Eleusís-Corinth highway, 26km northwest of Athens. Tel: (210) 5546 019. Open: Tue–Sun 8.30am–3pm. Admission charge.

Elevtheraí

This 4th-century BC Athenian fortress guards the pass between the Pateras and Kitheron ranges through which the former National Road between Athens and Thebes still runs. One massive wall of grey limestone blocks still stands, and goats shelter in the ruins of its towers.
Signposted to the north of the Athens–Thebes highway, 1km north of the Pórto Germeno turning. Free access.

Pórto Yermenó (Porto Germeno)

This delightful, quiet little resort at the head of an arm of the Korinthiakós Kólpos (Gulf of Corinth) seems more remote than it is. Ringed by steep, pine-covered slopes, it has a crescent of pebbly beach, busy only on summer weekends, and a handful of guesthouses and fish restaurants.
Signposted from Athens–Thebes highway, 71km northwest of Athens.

Nearby

The once-mighty Athenian fortress of **Aigósthena**, built in the 4th century BC as part of the defences on the Theban border, lies about 500m from Pórto

Yermenó village. Its massive walls ring a low hilltop, and five of its 15 square towers are still standing.

Thívai (Thebes)

A ruined 13th-century Frankish tower stands atop the hill which was the acropolis of ancient Thebes, one of the most powerful of the city-states. Allied with the Persians against Athens in 480 BC, Thebes remained a rival until Sparta defeated Athens in the Peloponnesian War. Thebes' finest hour came in 371 BC when it defeated Sparta to become chief of the Hellenic states. It was destroyed by Alexander in 336 BC. The main point of interest today is the **Mousío Thivai Arkheologiko (Thebes Archaeological Museum)** located right next to the castle. Its collection includes a 6th-century BC *kouros*, some unique black tombstones, and Mycenaean sarcophagi.
Thebes is 81km northwest of Athens. Thebes Archaeological Museum: Tel: (226) 202 7913. Open: Tue–Sun 8.30am–3pm. Admission charge.

Battlefields of Northern Attica
Three great battles for ancient Greece were fought in northern Attica. At Thermopylae (480 BC), the pass connecting Attica and Thessaly, 300 Spartans under King Leonidas fought to the death against a much larger Persian force. They were avenged at Plataiaí (479 BC) by a Greek alliance. At Lévktra (371BC) Thebes defeated mighty Sparta. There is little to see at the battlefields, but a statue of Leonidas stands near the site of Thermopylae, beside the OE1 highway.
Lévktra Signposted 12km south of Thebes.
Plataiaí Signposted 17km south of Thebes.
Thermopylae Signposted near Kamena Vourla on OE1 highway.

Tour: Attika and Ákra Soúnion

The best way to see the countryside and the superb archaeological sites of Attica is by car. The high point of the tour is the magnificent Temple of Poseidon at Ákra Soúnion (Cape Soúnion), on the very southern tip of the Attica peninsula.

Starting from central Athens, the tour covers 180km.
Allow 4 to 6 hours driving.

Leave Athens by the main coast highway, passing through the seaside suburbs of Glifádha, Voúla and Vouliagméni. On a clear day the island of Aíyina can be seen to the west, and the waters of the Saronikós Kólpos (Saronic Gulf) are dotted with yachts and ferries.

At Várkiza, set on a scenic bay with a pay beach managed by the Greek National Tourist Organisation, turn inland, following the signs to Vari (2km), then turn right in the direction of Koropi.

Leaving the urban sprawl of Athens, the countryside is much scarred by marble quarrying. At the Koropi crossroads, take the second right, which is signposted to

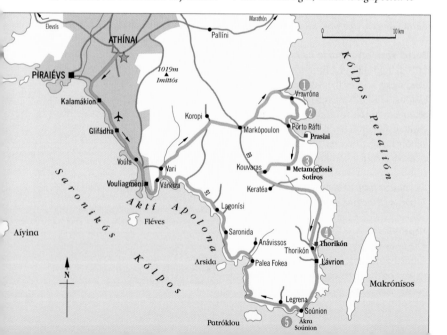

Markópoulon, and drive through prettier surroundings of rolling hills dotted with olive trees and vineyards.

At Markópoulon, follow signs first to Vravróna to visit the ancient temple site and museum, then to Pórto Ráfti. The road crosses a fertile plain covered with vineyards which sell their produce to the Kourtaki retsina winery in Markópoulo. The green vines are striking against the barren hillsides around them.

After 7km turn right, following signs to Vravróna and Pórto Ráfti. 250m from the turning you will see the columns of ancient Vravróna (see p49) on the left.

1 Vravróna

The sanctuary was dedicated to the goddess Artemis and dates from the 5th century BC. The site is shared by a 6th-century AD Christian basilica and the 15th-century chapel of Áyios Yioryios.
From Vravróna the road climbs through pine woods, descending to the sea after 3km.

2 Pórto Ráfti

The spectacularly located port and beach resort of Pórto Ráfti, on a broad, almost-enclosed blue bay, is a lovely place to stop for a snack and a swim.
Leaving Pórto Ráfti turn right (signposted to Kouvaras), and keep right. The road climbs through a pine-wooded valley.

3 Monastery of Metamórfosis Sotíros (Metamórphosis Sotiros)

The stately terracotta domes and bell towers of the monastery of Metamórphosis Sotiros (Transformation of the Saviour) stand guard over its olives and vines, surrounded by cypresses and palms.

The road zigzags through hills before joining the main road to Lávrion, which is soon bypassed for Cape Soúnion. Detour to the ancient site at Thorikón (signposted 'Theatre Antique' to the right of the road just before you enter Lávrion).

4 Thorikón (Thorikos)

An unusual oval-shaped theatre, seating 5,000, is currently being excavated at this hillside site, which dates from the 5th century BC.

5 Cape Soúnion

Homer's 'sacred headland' is crowned by the Temple of Poseidon, set atop 60-m high sea-cliffs, one of the most spectacular of Greece's ancient sites. The islands of Makrónisos and Kea float on the eastern horizon. The temple was built between 444 and 440 BC and restored in the 19th century. Its clifftop position was invaluable in war and it was at one time fortified. It was built as a tribute to the sea god Poseidon at a time of growing Athenian naval power.
Head back to Várkiza and Athens by the winding corniche road which follows the bays and headlands of the Apollo Coast. The drive back takes around 1 hour.

Mount Parnitha dominates the Athens skyline and offers escape from the summer heat

Pelopónnisos
The Peloponnese

Separated from the northern mainland by the Korinthiakós Kólpos (Gulf of Corinth), the Peloponnese is rich in history and in natural beauty. Its coasts have some of Greece's longest sandy beaches and prettiest remote coves, its mountains offer unrivalled views, and it is dotted with numerous ancient palaces, castles and fortresses spanning 5,000 years.

Typical strong bust of a Spartan warrior

The Isthmus of Corinth connects the Peloponnese with the northern mainland, and is cut across by the Dióriga Korínthou (Corinth Canal). Much of the region is mountainous, with one mighty chain of peaks, culminating in the Taïyetos summit, running down the centre.

Nowhere else is Greece's many-layered history so clearly on show. The northeast corner of the region was the cradle of the Mycenaean civilisation celebrated by Homer. The classical

The Arcadian Gate at Ancient Messini – testament to the monumental engineering skills of Sparta's great rival

and Hellenistic eras which followed are represented by Sparta, Corinth, Epídhavros and other sites.

The Byzantines built the fairy-tale castle of Mistra, above the Evrótas valley. Frankish princes left castles on a dozen hilltops. The Venetians fortified Návplion and Monemvasía and built grim strongholds at Methóni and Koróni. The Turks added yet another layer of history.

The Peloponnese is the birthplace of modern Greece. Here the War of Independence began in 1821, and here its fiercest battles were fought for possession of castles built

The Peloponnese

hundreds of years earlier. Together with Athens and the Sterea Ellas, the Peloponnese was the nucleus of the new Greek state established in 1830.

The north coast between Corinth and Patras is backed by steeply rising mountain slopes. West of Patras, the coast is dominated by long, sandy beaches, washed by the Ionian Sea across which lies Italy. Inland, every pass through the mountains is guarded by a medieval castle or classical temple, but one of the magnets for visitors is the magical site of ancient Olympia.

Each of the three peninsulas has its own aura: Akritas, with its Venetian fortresses, Taínaron with its deserted towers and Maléa with its empty hillsides.

On the east coast, some charmingly remote towns, villages and untouched beaches are cut off from the hinterland of the Peloponnese by the bulk of Párnon Óros (Mount Parnon).

The plays performed in theatres like Epídhavros were far more than mere entertainment. They began as religious experiences, and their purpose was to explain the ways of gods to men. They also, however, often commented on society and politics in the city. Later, the works of the great Greek dramatists influenced Roman theatre, and later still they inspired generation after generation of Western playwrights, including Shakespeare and his 16th- and 17th-century contemporaries. Modern theatre is still in their debt.

To the playwrights of ancient Athens, a comedy was more than merely a play to make people laugh, and a tragedy more than just a tear-jerker. Essentially, tragedy dealt with deeper religious or moral themes, and comedy with everyday affairs, but both forms were highly stylised and conventional. Actors were disguised in masks which portrayed their character's attributes and an on-stage chorus provided a running commentary.

Tragedies were presented in Athens at great annual festivals and were surrounded by splendid rituals. Every citizen (that is, every free-born Athenian man) was entitled and expected to attend.

Writers had a solemn social and religious responsibility and the most successful were richly rewarded.

The plot was less important than the exposition of the dramatist's theme, since the audience was already familiar with the story-line. Athenian audiences, in particular, instead wanted to see how a new play interpreted an old story, and one purpose of the drama was to keep alive tales which were a central part of Greek culture. Though described as 'hard to analyse, impossible to translate', the ancient plays of writers like the tragedians Sophocles (496–406 BC), Aeschylus (c.525–456 BC) and Euripides (484–406 BC), and the comedian Aristophanes (448–380 BC), are re-enacted each year at festivals in Athens and Epídhavros (see pp148–9). These can be moving events, especially if you have an English translation of the script, and their themes and even their humour are as relevant and fresh today as when they were written.

Works of the great Greek dramatists were performed at the great Theatre of Epídhavros (left); classical Greek actors, masks were made to show various emotions (above)
Below: bust of Sophocles by an unnamed German artist

Magnificently sited, the theatre at Epídhavros is a fitting location for Greek drama

THE ARGOLID

The Argolid is a blunt peninsula pointing southeast into the Aegean. The peninsula and the fertile plain at its landward end are rich in ancient and medieval sites.

There are beach resorts at Tolón, 4km from Návplion, and Portokhéli, on the peninsula's southern tip.

Árgos

The oldest continuously inhabited town in Europe – it was founded in 2000 BC – stands amid olive and citrus groves, a grid of modern buildings surmounted by Larissa Castle 300m above.

Kástro Lárissis (Larissa Castle)

The 13th-century Frankish Kástro Larissis (Larissa Castle) is impressive from below and ghostly within, as only the outer walls and the shell of the inner keep survive, but there are fine views south down the east coast.

Signposted, with access from the west side of the crag, 5km from the town centre. Free access.

Mousío Arkheologikoú (Archaeological Museum)

The museum contains minor finds from ancient Argos, including pottery, weapons and mosaics and a suit of 8th-century BC bronze armour.

*Town centre. Tel: (275) 102 8819.
Open: Tue–Sun 8.30am–3pm.
Admission charge.*

Nearby

Impressive remains of the 2nd-century AD Roman baths are to be found, along with the ruins of the largest theatre in

Greece (capacity 20,000), on Gounaris, the road to Tripoli.

Epídhavros

Set in a landscaped site among pines, the restored 4th-century BC theatre is the finest in Greece, seating 14,000 in 55 tiers, and is the main remnant of a sanctuary dedicated to Asklepios, the god of healing. Attending the theatre was thought to be beneficial to the spirit and the structure is still in use for the Epídhavros Festival from June to August each year, when the ancient plays are brought to life by its magnificent acoustics – you can clearly hear someone speaking in a normal voice, or even tearing a sheet of paper, from the top row of seats almost 23m above the stage. Only foundations remain of other buildings, though some of the tiered seats of the stadium still survive.

Archaeological Site and Museum:
Tel: (275) 302 2009. 28km east of
Návplion and 3km from the village of
Ligoúrion (Lygourion). Open: summer,
8am–7pm; winter, 8am–5pm.
Admission charge.

Iréon (Ireo)

Cyclopean blocks and column sections litter the site of the Sanctuary of Hera, the earth goddess of Argos. Tiers of walls and foundations give a clear view of the ground plan, but there are no signs to help make sense of the site, which is best appreciated from its highest point, the flagstoned floor of the 7th-century BC Doric Temple of Hera.

Ireo Archaeological Site, 2km north of
Inaxon, signposted erratically. Open: daily
8.30am–3pm. Free admission.

Mikínai (Mycenae)

The most impressive of the Argolid's dramatic ancient sites, excavated by the German Heinrich Schliemann (1822–90) in 1876.

He first found the ramparts, then a circle of royal tombs. The corpses found in them were decked in golden masks (including the famous so-called 'Mask of Agamemnon') and bracelets, now in the National Archaeological Museum in Athens.

Pass through the ramparts by the Lion Gate with its carved lionesses. Immediately within, to the right, are the first tombs discovered, dating from the 16th century BC. Below these and outside the walls is a second tomb circle, excavated in 1951 and dating from the 17th century BC. Next to this is the so-called Tomb of Clytemnestra, a 14th-century BC domed royal grave. Above the tombs, the tiers of the Royal Palace are connected by zigzagging marble stairs rising to a fortified acropolis.

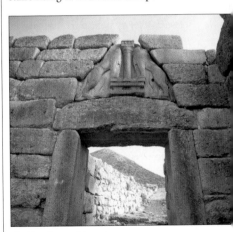
The Lion Gate at Mycenae

One of Mycenae's beehive tombs, discovered in recent times

Opposite the main site is the splendid Treasury of Atreus, a 13th-century BC beehive tomb over 13m high, quarried out of the hillside.

The site is 2km from modern Mikínai, signposted 7km southeast of the main Corinth–Argos road.

Archaeological Site and Treasury of Atreus: Tel: (275) 107 6585. Open: daily, summer 8am–7pm, winter 8am–5pm. Admission charge.

Návplion

A delightful harbour town whose shuttered stucco façades date from Návplion's brief 19th-century moment of glory as free Greece's first capital.

Akronavplíon (Its Kale)

A rugged ring of impressive Turkish-Venetian ramparts on the site of an earlier Frankish stronghold occupies a headland above the harbour. The Byzantine gatehouse has fine frescoes dated to AD 1291. The main area of the old citadel is now a hotel.

Boúrtzi

A quaint miniature fortress built by the Venetians in 1471, with a six-sided tower, adorns the island in the middle of Návplion's harbour. It also served in the past as a prison and the local hangman's home, but is now deserted.

Palamídhi

Built on the heights between 1711 and 1714, when the town was Venice's regional capital, the imposing stronghold is entered through gateways bearing the Lion of St Mark. The view from the top is magnificent.

Palamidhi Fortress. Tel: (275) 202 8036. Open: weekdays 8am–5pm, weekends & holidays 8.30am–3pm. Admission charge.

Tiryns

'Cyclopean' limestone boulder walls, up to 7m high and 700m in circumference, led later Greeks to believe that this 13th-century BC stronghold was built not by men but by giants like the one-eyed Cyclops of the myths. It is, in fact, the finest surviving example of Mycenaean military architecture. Historians estimate that the original height of the walls may have been as much as 20m – they are 10m thick in places. Little is known of the builders or of the ruling family, but it is

Palamidhi's formidable fortress

clear that the fortress suffered a violent end, the palace within being gutted by fire well before the classical period.

The fort is 4km north of Návplion. Tel: (275) 202 2657. Open: daily, summer 8am–7pm; winter 8am–3pm. Admission charge.

The island fortress of Bourtzi

'I have gazed upon the face of Agamemnon.'
HEINRICH SCHLIEMANN, 1876

In 1871 the German archaeologist Heinrich Schliemann staggered the world by finding proof that Homer's epics were more than myth. Inspired by the *Iliad*, he discovered the site of Troy near Canakkale in western Turkey. Three years later he made his first tentative excavations at Mycenae, and after two years, uncovered the palace and tombs containing gold-bedecked skeletons, one of them wearing the breathtaking golden mask now in the National Archaeological Museum in Athens. His discovery began an archaeologists' gold rush to excavate the rich sites surrounding Mycenae and ushered in a golden age of archaeological discovery.

The Mycenaeans were a Bronze-Age people who came to Greece from Asia around 2100 BC, and over the next five centuries they created a world of tiny kingdoms ruled from hilltop palaces built of crude but imposing massive stone blocks. They settled throughout southern Greece and established colonies in the islands and overseas, trading with the great empires of Egypt and the Middle East and with the Minoans of Crete. This first Greek civilisation fell quite suddenly around 1200 BC, leaving a treasury of finely-detailed figurines of people, gods and animals in bronze, gold and ceramics, elaborate seals and frescoes depicting scenes from everyday life, and gorgeous golden grave-goods. The later Dorian Greeks, who settled among the mighty ruins of the Mycenaean civilisation, wove a tapestry of legend around the dimly-remembered Mycenaeans and their palaces, kings and heroes.

Above: Heinrich Schliemann; left: Mycenaean pottery
Facing page: angels celebrate Homer's *Iliad* and *Odyssey*

Homer's Heroes

In one of the greatest stories ever told, the blind poet Homer wrote, probably in the 8th century BC, about events which were already far in the past. Homer drew on earlier folk tales for the basic plot and characters of his epics, the *Iliad* and the *Odyssey*, which deal with the 10-year siege of Troy, in Asia Minor, by a league of Mycenaean kings and princes from the Greek mainland and islands.

The war began when Paris, younger son of King Priam of Troy, ran off with the beautiful Helen, wife of King Menelaus of Sparta. Menelaus summoned his allies – the mighty warrior and commander Agamemnon, king of Mycenae; Nestor, wise old king of Pilos and a skilled charioteer; cunning Odysseus, ruler of Ithaca; and the invincible Achilles, dipped by his mother in a sacred spring to protect him against all weapons. Homer's *Iliad* deals with the last year of the siege during which Achilles was killed by an arrow which pierced his ankle, his only vulnerable spot.

In the Aeneid, the Roman poet Virgil (70–19 BC) tells how Troy fell not to the valour of Achilles but to a ruse. The Greeks built a giant wooden horse, which they left as an offering to Poseidon when the fleet sailed away. The Trojans dragged it into the city, not knowing that Greek warriors lurked within. That night, the fleet returned, the hidden commandos emerged to open the gates, and the city fell.

ÁKRA AKRITAS (CAPE AKRITAS)
Anáktora Nestoros (Palace of Nestor)

It is hard to picture the 13th-century BC palace of the great elder statesman of the Trojan War from its mud and stone foundations, but the site has a fine view across Navarino Bay. There is a cavernous 13th-century BC beehive tomb about 100m from the palace site.

17km north of Pílos.
Tel: (276) 303 1437.
Open: Tue–Sun
8.30am–3pm.
Admission charge.

Kástro Ton Paramythion (Castle of the Fairy-tales)

Winged horses, 5-m high stucco statues and tableaux from Greek history surround the extraordinary three-storey folly with its red and yellow spires and white plaster battlements built in the 1950s by the late Dr Haralambos Fournarakis.

On the shore, between Kiparissía and Filiatrá. From Kiparissía, follow signs to Agrili. The building is not open to the public.

Kiparissía

A pocket-sized Byzantine castle sits crumbling on a pine-covered hilltop above this farming and fishing town, which spreads between the coastal hills and a long strip of pebbly beach.

1km from town centre.

Koróni

The lovely castle at Koróni looks east to the summits of Taïyetos (Taiyetos) and the cliffs of Outer Mani, and down on to the red roofs, esplanade and palm trees of the town itself. Koróni and Methóni, known in the Middle Ages as 'the Eyes of Venice', guarded the sea routes to Venice's eastern colonies. To the south, you can see Koróni's one-kilometer sweep of sandy beach.

The ramparts surround houses, gardens, and a cemetery and monastery among pines and olives.

500m from the esplanade.
Free access.

Methóni

A fortified city from a historical romance, Methóni occupies a headland jutting into a vast bay, sheltered by the island of Sapiéntza, protected to landward by impregnable walls and a deep moat. Within, a 750-m cobbled

NAVARINO

The calm bay, sheltered by the islands of Navarino and Sfaktiria has always attracted seafarers to Pílos, from King Nestor, the elder statesman of the *Iliad* and the *Odyssey*, Homer's epics of the Trojan War, to Venetian and Turkish fleets in medieval and modern times.

On 20 October 1827, a Turkish fleet, anchored in the bay, was sunk by a flotilla of British, French and Russian ships commanded by the British Admiral Lord Codrington. Codrington's instructions were to observe, but when the Turks fired on one of the allied ships they responded in kind. The sinking of the Turkish fleet helped to decide the War of Independence in favour of the Greeks.

road leads from the inner keep past ruined mosques and churches, cracked spires and toppling arches to the octagonal Bourtzi tower on an island connected by a causeway. The Lion of St Mark, symbol of Venice, is emblazoned on the stonework to the left of the main gate, close to the sea. Sunset over the Bourtzi is best viewed from the long sandy beach east of the castle. Modern Methóni, outside the walls, is a lively tourist resort in summer, reverting to a somnolent farming and fishing town out of season.

63km southwest of Kalamata. The castle overlooks Methóni harbour.
Tel: (273) 102 5363. Open: Tue–Sun 8.30am–3pm. Admission charge.

Pílos

The peaceful town of white- and cream-painted 19th-century houses overlooking the lagoon-like bay of Navarino is built around a small harbour (slated for development as a marina), guarded by the huge Neo Kástro.
51km west of Kalamata.

Neo Kástro (New Castle)

The castle was built by the Turks in the late 16th century to control the bay of Navarino and counter the Venetian forts at Methóni and Koróni. Recently restored, it contains a small museum with a fine collection of prints and lithographs of heroes of the War of Independence. The etching *Lendemain de Navarin* (The Day After Navarino) shows a disconsolate Turk clinging to a spar among the wreckage of his fleet.
Above Pílos, 500m from the harbour.
Tel: (272) 302 2010. Open: daily 8.30am–3pm. Admission charge.

Only the stone foundations of the Palace of Nestor survived a fire in the 12th century BC

THE CENTRAL PELOPONNESE

The heartland of the Peloponnese is a blend of rugged mountains, rolling hills and farming valleys filled with olive trees.

Andrítsaina (Andhritsaina)

A charming, old-fashioned hill town surrounded by barren peaks, Andhritsaina rises from a main square dominated by an enormous plane tree, and in summer is full of café tables. Many of its older houses have tiled roofs and overhanging second storeys.
65km from Tripolis.

Karítaina

Commanding the Alfiós valley, the 13th-century baronial castle of the Frankish de Bruyères family balances precariously above the half-deserted medieval village. Halfway up the steep path to the citadel stands a marble bust, erected in 1939, of Theodoros Kolokotronis, the great general whose forces garrisoned the castle in the 1821–30 War of Independence.
55km from Tripolis.
Free access.

Mantinéia

Founded in about 500 BC, Mantineia was destroyed by the Spartans in 385 BC and rebuilt in 371 BC when Thebes was victorious over Sparta. The ruins date from the 371 rebuilding, and of particular interest are the massive town walls, over 4m thick and almost 4km in length, with 10 gates and 120 towers.
11km north of Tripolis on the main road to Olympia. Free access.

Megalópolis (Magalopoli)

Relics of the ancient city, built between 371 and 368 BC by Epaminondas of Thebes to curb the power of Sparta, include the foundations of the 66m by 53m assembly hall and the lower rows of a 59-tier theatre which seated nearly 20,000.
Signposted one km north of the modern town of Magalopoli on the Karitaina road.
Open: Tue–Sun 8.30am–3pm. Free admission.

Trípolis

The quiet market town of Tripolis is the hub of the Peloponnese road and rail networks, and the gateway to the more exciting

THE FRANKS OF THE MOREA

In 1204 the Frankish soldiers of the Fourth Crusade turned on the Byzantine Empire, sacked Constantinople, and carved the empire (of which Greece was then part) into a federation of Latin kingdoms. One of these knights, Geoffrey de Villehardouin, took the Peloponnese, then called Achaía or the Morea, dividing it into 12 baronies which he gave to his followers. The Frankish barons occupied and added to Byzantine castles such as Acrocorinth and Monemvasía, or built new ones like Karitaina and Mistra. The Latin mini states in Greece lasted just half a century before being driven out by a newly assertive Byzantium.

In 1259 the Frankish knight William de Villehardouin was defeated by the exiled Byzantine emperor. Two years later, the Byzantines reconquered Constantinople and gradually drove the Franks from their remaining strongholds.

southern Peloponnese. The town stands amid farmland on a 600m plateau ringed by mountains. It suffered heavy damage from the Turks under General Ibrahim Pasha during the War of Independence. It is a far cry from the holiday hotspots and a good place to come if you want to see everyday Greek life unaffected by the tourism business. *180km southwest of Athens.*

Vassái

The dramatically sited **Temple of Apollo Epikourios** (Apollo the Succourer) at Vassai stands 1,128m above sea level, looking out over the blue slopes of the Arkadian mountain ranges. The temple's tottering pillars are braced by a web of scaffolding and it is protected from the elements by a vast high-tech marquee. Built in 450–420 BC, it is one of the best preserved of the ancient temples and is attributed to Iktinos, one of the builders of the Parthenon. It was rediscovered, almost intact, by the French architect and archaeologist Joachim Bocher in 1765. Like those of the Parthenon, its

Precarious wooden balconies overhang Andhritsaina's streets

friezes were acquired by the British Museum in the early 19th century and are still exhibited in London.

With 15 Doric columns on its long sides and six on each end, the temple is much narrower than is common and, unusually, is oriented north to south instead of east to west.
Signposted 65km southeast from Olympia. Free access.

The main square in Andhritsaina where a large plane tree provides shelter from the sun

CORINTH AND AROUND
Arkhéa Kórinthos (Ancient Corinth)

Corinth's varying fortunes through the ages are reflected in the ruins of the ancient city, which span 800 years, from the 5th century BC to the 3rd century AD. A great power in the 8th century BC, Corinth was later overshadowed by Athens until again ascendant as chief of the League of Corinth under the Macedonian kings. In Roman times the city was one of the great imperial cities, but the fall of Rome, barbarian invasions and Turkish conquest eventually obliterated it. Ancient Corinth is actually situated at the foot of the hill of Akrokórinthos (Acrocorinth), 7km southwest of the modern city.

Highlights of the site are the Temple of Apollo, with seven of its 38 Doric columns intact, dating from the 6th century BC, and the Peirene Fountain with its stone arches and colonnade. Other relics include the 150m by 90m site of the Agorá and the foundations of the enormous *stoa* which occupied its south side. The seats of a small Roman *odeon*, carved from the rock in the 1st century AD, are clearly visible next to the much larger 18,000-seat theatre built in the 5th century BC and enlarged in the 3rd century BC by the Romans, who used it for gladiatorial contests.

The museum features Roman mosaics and statues, pottery and several small bronzes.

Ancient Corinth is signposted 7km south-west of modern Corinth.
Archaeological Site and Museum:
Tel: (274) 103 1207. Open: daily, summer 8am–8pm; winter 8am–3pm.
Admission charge includes both.

The Corinth Canal, 23m wide and 6km long

Akrokórinthos (Acrocorinth)

Towering on its 500m crag above the site of ancient Corinth, the immense ramparts of this medieval stronghold embrace Ancient Greek, Roman, Frankish and Turkish remnants. A Byzantine fortress, it was taken by the Franks in 1211 and added to by Frankish princes over the next 180 years. It passed back to Byzantium in 1394 and was later held by the Knights of St John, the Venetians and the Turks. The 15th-century ramparts, 3km long, are pierced by three gates, and inside there are two more walls built by the Byzantines. Within the walls are a dilapidated mosque and minaret, and a small church among the tumbled walls of the Turkish town. Beside the minaret is an ancient well, still providing water.

From the highest point, marked by a

Corinthian capital atop a concrete pillar, there are awe-inspiring 360-degree views.
Acrocorinth Archaeological Site.
Tel: (274) 103 1207. Two km above the archaeological site of ancient Corinth.
Open: daily, summer 8.30am–7pm; winter 8.30am–3pm.
Free admission.

Dióriga Korínthou (Corinth Canal)

The Corinth Canal, begun by a French company in 1882 and completed by the Greeks 11 years later, is today more a landmark than a shipping route. The canal helped make Piraeus Greece's major port, but it is too narrow for modern vessels and is used only by smaller cruise ships. It is 6.3km long, 23m wide and 80m below the land surface, and crossed by two bridges, the eastern one carrying the Athens-Patras National Road.

Several rulers of the region in ancient times (the Roman Emperor Nero among them) attempted to build a canal across the isthmus, though none succeeded. The Greek allies built a wall across the isthmus in 480 BC to keep the Persians out, which remained in place until Venetian times. The Venetians and the Turks found it a useful source of stone and no sign of it survives.
On the main Patras-Athens highway.

Kórinthos (Corinth)

Modern Corinth, repeatedly levelled by earthquakes (the most recent in 1981) is a modern seaside town which can be bypassed en route to the ancient site. There is little of interest here, though the town has plenty of shops and a few restaurants.

DEEP MÁNI

Deep Máni, a mountainous finger of land protected by cliffs and easily defended narrow passes, was never fully under Turkish control. The Maniot clans were virtually self-governing and spent their time feuding with each other from their tiny square castles when not allied in rebellion against Turkey. Feuds went on not only from village to village but between families in the same village, and rivals strove to build the tallest towers.

Areópolis

Once resounding to the shouts and gunfire of the Mavromichalis clan, this now quiet village is where the War of Independence against Turkish occupation began.
26km west of Yíthion.

Kelefá

The huge, empty grey shell of Kelefá Castle, built in the 17th century by the Turks to control the turbulent clans,

Mountains hover over a Deep Máni village

guards the gateway to Deep Máni. To the north the village of Itilon stands beneath the grim peaks called the Pendadaktylos (the five-fingered).
Signposted 4km northwest from the Areópolis-Yíthion road on a rough track. Free access.

Kíta

Once the largest and most powerful of the towered villages, Kita looks from a distance like a miniature city of skyscrapers, but most of its towers have fallen into picturesque disrepair.
16km south of Areopolis.

Kótronas

Ringed by steep rocky slopes, this out-of-the-way harbour village with a

small stretch of east-facing pebbly beach sits at the end of a fjord-like bay.
40km south of Yíthion.

Passavá

The battlements of the 13th-century Frankish castle, now in ruins, can be seen from the Yíthion-Areópolis road only with difficulty (*see* Inner Máni and Ákra Taínaron tour, *pp80–81*).
11km south of Yíthion.

Pórto Káyio (Porto Kaigio)

The tarred road ends here, at one of the prettiest unspoiled bays in Greece. Once famous for its game birds – its name means 'Port of Quails' – it is still a favourite with locals during the

Market day at Areópolis

Scenic villages line the Deep Máni coast

Boats ready for the river journey through the Dhirou caverns

autumn hunting season.
65km south of Yíthion.

Spílaion Dhiroú/Dhirou Spilies (Dhirou Caves)

A 1.2km river flows through the Vlychadha Cavern, a wonderland of spires, cones, needles and stalactites. The tour by boat takes 30 minutes. The museum displays neolithic finds from the Alepotripa cave, still being explored.
7km west from the Areópolis-Yerolimín main road, signposted from Pirgos Dhirou. Tel: (273) 305 2222. Open: Jun–Sep, daily 8am–6pm; rest of the year 8am–3pm. Admission charge. Museum open: daily 8.30am–3pm. Separate admission charge.

Taínaron

South of Porto Kaigio the potholed road runs through rugged, semi-desert scenery to end abruptly above the site of the 5th-century BC Temple of Poseidon, in a cave said to be one of the entrances to Hades, the land of the dead. The cave, little more than a depression in the rock, now houses donkeys and nothing remains of the temple. To the right, past a tiny pebble cove, the rough path passes the remains of a circular mosaic floor, exposed to the elements. Follow the path southwest over the headland to the Taínaron lighthouse and the southern tip of Greece, where cliffs plunge to dazzling azure water.
7km south of Pórto Káyio.

Váthia

Still ruinous but making a comeback thanks to tourism, the spectacular tower village of Váthia, atop a cactus-covered hill, is the best preserved of the Mani tower villages. Surrounded by bare hillsides, it is full of old houses and medieval bastions and keeps.
9km southeast from the port of Yerolimín.

THE EAST COAST
Ákra Maléa (Cape Malea)
Easternmost of the peninsulas of the
southern Peloponnnese, mountainous
Ákra Maléa (Cape Malea) points towards
the island of Kíthira on the southern
horizon. The cape's eastern side is rocky
and inaccessible, and the main road
ends about 11km south of Monemvasía.

Kiparissía
The white villas and cottages of
Kiparissia stand among the cypress trees
which give it its name, above a sweep of
pebbly beach. The imposing slopes of
the Párnon massif rise almost vertically
behind the village.
40km north of Monemuasia.

Leonídhion
Precarious balconies overhang the
streets of this pleasantly unchanged
small town at the foot of a dizzyingly
steep canyon running far into the
mountains. Leonídhion stands 3km
inland from its harbour and beach, the
former a favourite with yacht sailors and
the latter a magnet for holidaying
Athenians. Between the pebbly, 1-km
long beach and the town is a delta of
fertile farmland dotted with fruit trees,
olive groves and colourful plantations of
peppers, aubergines and tomatoes.
68km south of Navplion.

Monemvasía
The dizzying 300-m high rock of
Monemvasía, 400m offshore, is a natural
fortress, added to by Byzantine,
Frankish, Venetian and Turkish builders.
It gives its name to malmsey wine,
exported from the Aegean islands to

The island fortress at Monemvasía, the Gibraltar
of Greece

Europe by the Venetians. The name
means 'one entrance', and with its cliffs
and ramparts Monemvasía looks like a
tough proposition for any belligerent
besieger.

In fact, it was frequently conquered
when the defenders ran out of water.
Populous until the early 19th century, it
was taken and sacked by the Greeks
during the War of Independence and the
last permanent resident of the cragtop
fortress died in 1906.

The settlement on the rock and on the
mainland opposite falls into three parts:
the Kástro, Pano Kástro and Yefira.
100km southeast of Sparta.

Kástro (Castle)
The lower town, within the medieval
walls, is a maze of arches, alleys, steps
and tall 15th-century Venetian houses,
many of them restored as hotels or
holiday apartments. Strict rules ensure
that houses are rebuilt in traditional
style, and no vehicles can pass the iron-
bound gates through the medieval walls.
Even in high summer you can wander
through cobbled lanes lined with
crumbling walls and wild fig trees

without meeting another soul, though in its medieval heyday it had a population of 30,000 and as many as 40 churches.

Páno Kástro (Upper Castle)

The early medieval town on the flat top of the crag is a honeycomb of shattered walls and collapsed archways. The only intact building is the late 13th-century church of Áyia Sofia, with some interesting frescoes.

Yefíra (Bridge)

The modern fishing and tourism town on the mainland takes its name from the causeway and bridge which connect it with the castle. Restaurants and cafés surround the harbour and there is a pebbly beach to the north. There is a sandier beach, with fine views of the castle rock, at Pori, 3km north of Yefira on the main road.

Paralía Astros

The shell of a Frankish castle on a headland overlooks a yacht and fishing harbour at the north end of a 2km crescent of sandy, pebbly beach. Behind the village, a mixture of 18th- and 19th-century stone houses below the castle and modern villas around the harbour, a sea of olives laps at the foothills of Parnon, 2km inland. Inland lies an immense freshwater lagoon ringed with reeds, a magnet for kingfishers, swans and wading birds.
30km south of Návplion.

Kástro (Castle)

The 15th-century castle at Paralia Astros has outstanding panoramic views down the east coast, across the Argolikos Kólpos (Argolic Gulf) and the island of Spétsai (Spetses), and north to Návplion.
On the hill above the town. Free access.

The Venetian bell tower within the lower Kástro at Monemvasía

THE EVROTAS VALLEY
Mistrás (Mistra)

The ultimate medieval fairy-tale castle, with a complex of ruined domes, palaces and ramparts surrounding a pinnacle on the east flank of Taiyetos, above modern Sparta. Fortified by the Villehardouin princes to seal the pass above it, Mistra passed into Byzantine hands after the battle of Pelagonia (1259) and held out against the Turks until 1460, seven years after the fall of Constantinople. It was repeatedly besieged during the struggles for control of the Peloponnese in the 16th and 17th centuries, and during the War of Independence, when it was finally burned and abandoned.

The site is crowned by a fortress on a crag, with steps and paths winding through the ruined buildings below, several of which are being restored. The most important buildings are the frescoed church of Áyia Sofia, immediately below the castle; the imposing four-storey Palace of the Despots; and Perívleptos, PanÁyia and Áyios Nikolaos churches. Near the main gate, a small museum exhibits a collection of column pedestals and fragments.

6km from Sparta, the lower Main Gate is 1km from the modern village of Mistras. The upper Fortress Gate is signposted 2km further uphill. Tel: (273) 1093 377. Open: daily 8am–3pm. Admission charge.

Spárti (Sparta)

Founded in 1836 by settlers made homeless by the destruction of Mistra in the War of Independence, modern Sparta shows little connection with the city-

Medieval Mistra

state which dominated the entire region from the 6th to the 4th century BC. Ancient Sparta depended for defence on the legendary courage and prowess of its warriors, not on fortifications, and, unlike their Athenian rivals, the Spartans built no great stone temples, monuments or public buildings. Modern Sparta is a pleasant enough market town set in breathtaking scenery, with the jagged, lunar summits of Taïyetos jostling for space on its western skyline.
60km south of Tripolis.

Mousío Arkheologikoú (Archaeological Museum)

Housed in an elegant neo-classical building in a statue-filled garden shaded by tall palms, the collection includes mosaics, marble reliefs from the 6th century BC, a bust of a Spartan warrior from 490–480 BC, a colossal Hellenistic head of Hercules, and a collection of scowling votive masks from the nearby Sanctuary of Artemis Orthia.
East side of Leoforos K Palaeoglou, between Evangelistrias and Lykourgos. Tel: (273) 102 5363. Open: Tue–Sun 8.30am–3pm. Admission charge.

Yeráki

The dramatic ruined fortress of Yeráki on its hilltop is visible far away across the flat bottom of the Evrotas valley, above the modern village of the same name. There is an awesome view of the saw-toothed Taÿetos, 20km west. The shattered shells of several small churches surround the castle walls.

4km east of Yeráki village, 1km from main road. Free access.

Yíthion

Close to the mouth of the wide, fertile Evrotas flood plain, Yíthion dozes by a mirror-calm harbour sheltered by Kranai, the island where Paris and Helen spent their first night of passion together before fleeing to Troy. Elegant old mansions with wrought-iron balconies mount in tiers above the port, relics of its 19th-century, when its fleet of schooners carried all the trade of the region.

48km south of Sparta.

Mousío Tzannetákis (Tzannetakis Museum)

This is a small museum situated in an 18th-century tower, devoted to the history of the Mani. Exhibits include books, writings and paintings.

On the island of Kranai, reached by a causeway from the harbour esplanade. Tel: (273) 302 2676.
Open: daily 9.30am–3pm.
Admission charge.

Arkaíou Théatrou (Ancient Theatre)

Built by the Romans in the 1st century AD, the compact theatre has 13 tiers of seats.

East end of Odhos Arkaiou Theatrou. Free access.

Mansions built by wealthy 19th-century shipowners line the harbour at Yíthion

ITHÓMI, KALÁMAI (KALAMATA) AND THE OUTER MANI
Ithomi (Ancient Messini/Messene)

A row of grim grey towers on a spur of Ithomi Oros (Mount Ithomi), remnant of a 10km ring of ramparts, guards the ruins of Ancient Messini, an agorá, theatre and stadium built in the 4th century BC. Messini, destroyed after rebelling against Sparta, was rebuilt by the Theban ruler Epaminondas after his defeat of Sparta at Leuktra in 379 BC. There is a fine aerial view of the site from the village of Mavromati, 300m above it. From the Lakonian Gate, 1.5km uphill from Mavromati, there is a panoramic view over the pastoral patchwork of the Messinian plain.

11km from modern Messini, and confusingly signposted Ancient Messini, Ithomi, Archaic Ithomi, Ancient Messini and Ithomi Archaeological Site.
Free access.

Kalámai (Kalamata)

The largest town in the southern Peloponnese with 40,000 inhabitants, Kalamata is of little interest to sightseers. The town was completely destroyed in the War of Independence and since then has been rocked by earthquakes several times, most recently in 1986.

Kardhamíli

This little town of sturdy 18th- and 19th-century balconied houses with its 2km beach of white pebbles and miniature harbour overlooking the **Messiniakos Kólpos** (Messinian Gulf) is the gateway to the Mani, a mountainous land of vendettas whose noble families

built themselves miniature castles from which to defy their rivals. One of these quaint square towers, the stronghold of the Mourtzinos family, can be seen at the ghost village of **Palaeo Kardhamíli** (Old Kardhamíli) nearby. It was built in 1808. Next to it stands a Byzantine church with an unusual stone spire decorated with a carved floral pattern.

30km southeast of Kalamata.
Palaeo Kardhamíli is 750m from the west end of Kardhamíli, signposted Old Kardamíli.

Stoúpa

A delightful, relaxed resort on a sheltered bay with a sandy crescent of west-facing beach, with Ákra Akritas on the horizon, backed by a dramatic landscape – the sheer, treeless and almost uninhabited slopes of the Taïyetos range.

35km southeast of Kalamata.

Thalámes

The square-built stone houses and antique pantiled Byzantine church of Thalames perch on a steep limestone hillside among olive groves and cypresses. Below it the slopes plunge away to pebbly coves and hidden beaches.

50km southeast of Kalamata.

Mousío Máni (Máni Museum)

This gloriously eclectic and eccentric collection of tools, weapons, furniture, banknotes, coins, books, portraits and posters should not be missed. The ground floor houses cases of potsherds, glassware and rusting swords and muskets, while the upper floor is decorated with naive posters depicting

Greece's struggles for independence.
On main street of the village, signposted.
Tel: (272) 107 4414.
Open: summer only, daily 9am–4pm.
Admission charge.

Taïyetos Óros (Mount Taïyetos)

Mount Taïyetos forms the jagged
backbone of the southern Peloponnese,
running from the centre of the province
to form the peninsula of Ákra Taínaron.
The western slopes of the massif are
barren, but its eastern flanks,
overlooking the Evrotas plain, are
cloaked in fir and pine. Atop its highest
peak, once sacred to Apollo, stands the
shrine of Profitis Ilias (Prophet Elijah),
the scene of a colourful annual festival
(18–20 July, *see* Festivals). The ascent to
the 2,407m peak can only be made on
foot and should be attempted only by
fit, experienced mountain walkers. The
summits of the range are snow-capped
as late as June.

Earthquakes

Southern Greece has been struck by
earthquakes throughout history, which
accounts for the ruinous state of many of
the ancient temples. Kalámai (Kalamata) has
been particularly unlucky, being rocked by
quake after quake over the last two
centuries. In September 1986 it was hit
again. Much of the damage has been
repaired with aid from the European
Community, but the town still has a shell-
shocked air.

Nine-km long stone walls once surrounded the ancient city of Messini, protecting it from rival Sparta

THE NORTH COAST AND ACHAÍA

Achaía Clauss

A charming mock-Bavarian castle in the hills is the headquarters of Greece's oldest winery. Founded in 1861 by Gustav Clauss (1825–1908), Achaía Clauss makes red and white table wines and dessert wines, all of which can be sampled and bought.

Signposted 5km from the centre of Patras. Tel: (261) 032 5051. Open: daily 11am–8pm. Free admission.

Chlemoútsi (Castle Tornese)

Round bastions and sheer walls surround the vaulted inner hall and courtyard of this hilltop stronghold. Built in 1220, it was the seat of Geoffrey II Villehardouin's princedom of Achaía, as this region is still called. From the ramparts, you can see the islands of Zákinthos and Kefallonia.

86km southwest of Patras, 4km from Kilini. Open: Tue–Sun 8.30am–5pm. Free admission.

Kalávrita

This leafy mountain village has a special significance for Greeks. Near here, in 1821, Archbishop Germanos called for the beginning of the War of Independence. Many of the inhabitants were martyred by the Germans in 1943 on suspicion of harbouring resistance fighters. Kalávrita's main attraction is the narrow-gauge railway running through a deep canyon to Diakofto, on the Gulf of Corinth (*see* The Dhiakoptón to Kalávrita Railway tour, *pp82–3*).

Killíni (Kilini)

A fishing harbour on the tip of a west-pointing headland, Kilini offers a long sandy beach and the opportunity of a day trip to Zákinthos.

Olimbía (Olympia)

The peaceful modern village of 900 people exists only to service visitors to ancient Olympia, the site of the Olympic Games for over 1,000 years. Most of the buildings on the archaeological site have been reduced to their foundations, but it is easy to picture the stadium packed with cheering crowds.

Altis (Sanctuary)

The sanctuary is the heart of Olympia and was sacred to the god Zeus. Its total area covered 200sq m.

The Doric Temple of Zeus, its most important structure, was demolished in the 6th century AD by an earthquake, though its ruins are still imposing. It was this temple that contained the huge statue of Zeus that was considered one of the Seven Wonders of the World.

Some columns of the neighbouring Temple of Hera have been rebuilt.

Ergasteirion (Workshop of Phidias)

Built for Phidias, the greatest sculptor of classical times, who worked on his statue of Zeus here. In Byzantine times it became a church.

Leonidhíon

Donated in the 4th century BC by Leonidas of Naxos, the Leonidhíon was a luxurious inn for the rulers and dignitaries who visited the games. The Romans added a central pool to its four wings of rooms around a courtyard.

Mousío (Museum)

The most striking exhibits are the helmet of Miltiades, the victor of Marathón, found buried beneath the stadium as an offering to Zeus; the superb friezes from the Temple of Zeus, representing the legendary battle between the Lapiths and Centaurs; and the statue of Hermes of about 350 BC, discovered in 1877.

Paléstra

A Hellenistic double colonnade surrounded this training arena, where wrestlers and other athletes sparred.

Stádion (Stadium)

The 193m course seated 20,000 – no women were admitted, except the priestess of Demeter, on pain of death.

Archaeological site, clearly signposted 2km from modern Olympia. Tel: (262) 402 2517. Open: daily, summer 8am–7pm; winter 8am–5pm.
Museum opposite archaeological site: Tel: (262) 402 2529, Open: daily, summer 8am–7pm; winter 8am–5pm. Admission charge includes site and museum.

Pátrai (Patras)

Greece's third largest city is the gateway to Greece for those arriving by sea from Italy. It was rebuilt after being virtually destroyed in World War II. The café-filled squares and avenues of the town centre are overlooked by a crumbling, 1,000-year-old castle.
212km west of Athens.

Áyios Andreas

The largest church in the Balkans, built in 1979 to house the gold casket containing the head of the saint, who was executed by the Romans in Patras, and which was returned to Patras from St Peter's by Pope Paul VI in 1964.
Platia Ayíou Andreou. Open: daily, except during services. Free admission.

Kástro (Castle)

The battlements of a 9th-century Byzantine castle with Frankish, Venetian and Turkish additions rise from the peak of a wooded hill close to the city centre.
Southeast end of Odhos Áyios, Nikolaou. Tel: (261)062 3390. Open: Tue–Sat 8am–5.30pm, Sun 8.30am–2pm.

Column bases of the Paléstra at Olympia, training ground for the competitors

Tour: Inner Máni and Ákra Taínaron

The Máni is dotted with castles, Byzantine churches and ruined towers. The 136km route follows newly built roads and is well signposted.
Allow 8 hours.

Leave Yíthion by the coast road towards Areópolis, passing the long beach of Mavrovoúni and then winding through wooded hills.

1 Passavá
The hilltop battlements of the 13th-century Frankish castle are hard to spot from the road. Look out for the signpost to Khosiarion (Xosiario), 9km after leaving Yíthion. Park at the Country Tavern (signposted in English) and pick your way up a very rough track. Only the walls still stand. Allow 1 hour.
A narrow pass ends in a fertile plain below the village of Vakhós (Vahos) and the bare flanks of Kouskouni.

2 Kelefá
Signposted to your right, 4km off the main road on a rough track (park by the village cemetery and walk the last 1km), Kelefá's mighty walls sheltered a strong Turkish garrison.
After 1km the main road emerges high above the west coast of the Máni, with the Messinian peninsula to the west.

3 Areópolis
The 'capital of the Máni' is ringed with tumbledown houses and fallen walls, but many old mansions are being restored as second homes.
The road south balances between desert mountains and sea cliffs on a fertile strip of olive groves and grainfields divided by dry-stone walls. At Pirgos Dhirou turn right (signposted Spilaia Dhirou/Caves) for 5km.

4 Spílaion Dhiroú (The Dhirou Caves)

Allow 25 minutes for the tour of the Vlychadha Cavern and underground river (*see p71*).

The main road bypasses a chain of half-ruined tower villages like clusters of miniature skyscrapers. At the hamlet of Áyios Yioryios look seaward for your first view of Tigáni. Turn right to Stavríon, a 4km detour, and park at the tiny collection of towers 1km beyond. A donkey track leads downhill to Tigáni. The walk is strenuous and involves picking your way among jagged boulders. Allow 1 hour.

5 Tigáni

The clifftop castle gets its name, which means 'frying pan', from the rocky peninsula it stands on. The handle of the frying pan is a natural causeway, making it a superb stronghold.
Return to the main coast road and turn right.

6 Tourlotí

To the left, 1.5km north of Kita and 300m above the new road, the 9th-century domed church of Tourlotí is one of the prettiest of dozens of Byzantine churches in the Máni.

7 Kíta

The largest tower village, Kíta was the seat of the Máni's most powerful clans. Tourism has brought some life back to the half-ruined village.
The sea is hidden by the Kavo Grosso plateau. After 5km the road descends to the half-abandoned harbour of Yerolimin, then winds through hills, passing through Alika.

8 Váthia

The towers of Váthia house a Greek National Tourist Organisation guesthouse (*see p177*). A tiny pebbly beach 1km below offers swimming.
Continue towards the cape.

9 Pórto Káyio and Ákra Taínaron

The lovely lagoon is overlooked by a tiny Turkish fort and is a favourite yacht anchorage.
Ákra Taínaron is 5km south and you must walk the final kilometre to Greece's southern tip (see p71).

Backtrack to Alika and turn right, cresting a pass 3km above Tsíkkaliá (Tsikalia). There are sweeping views of the Lakonikós Kólpos (Laconic Gulf) and Ákra Malea before the road plunges 300m to the sea at Kokkala and its pebbly white beach. It then follows the contours of the coast up to Kótronas and turns inland to Areópolis.

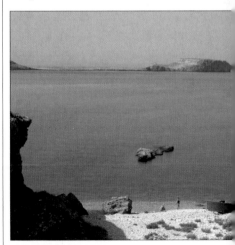

The barren peninsula of Tigáni is ringed by the ramparts of a Byzantine castle

Tour: The Dhiakoptón (Dhiakofton) to Kalávrita Railway

The narrow-gauge rack-and-pinion railway between Dhiakoptón, on the shores of the Gulf of Corinth and Kalávrita offers the most spectacular train ride in Greece, passing through a series of tunnels in a narrow mountain gorge. Originally drawn by tiny steam engines – one still stands at each of the two stations – the train is now driven by sturdy little French-built diesel locomotives which pull two carriages seating 68 people. First- and second-class seating is available. Six departures daily each way; no reservations needed.

The 23km journey takes 68 minutes each way. Allow 3 hours (4 if visiting the Mega Spileon Monastery).

Leaving Dhiakoptón the train rattles through lemon groves, passes under the busy National Road and enters the steep-sided Vouraïkós gorge.

Towering grey and pink limestone crags and sheer cliffs pocked with caves and holes loom above the track as the train climbs laboriously through pine woods. As the going gets steeper the rack-and-pinion gear is engaged and the train weaves in and out of a series of gallery tunnels, moving at little more than walking speed.

1 Zakhloroú (Zahlorou)

After about 40 minutes the tiled roofs and white houses of Zakhlorou emerge from the chestnut and cherry trees. The train stops here briefly for passengers wishing to visit the monastery at Mega

Spileon, which involves a steep, 45-minute walk.

2 Megálou Spilaíou (Mega Spileon)

Founded in the 8th century, when its miraculous icon of the Virgin was revealed to two monks by a shepherd girl, the monastery was rebuilt this century after a fire and its exterior is dull. Inside, the icon is surrounded by gold gift-offerings, watches, chains and rings, and you can just make out the frescoes painted on the sooty ceiling. The excellent small museum contains icons, holy relics and 18th- and 19th-century vestments, and is open daily (8am–1pm & 5pm–sunset; admission charge, small). Proper dress is necessary.

Miniature locomotive on the Dhiakoptón railway line

Kalávrita station is the southern terminus of the Dhiakoptón railway

Above Zakhlorou the slope is not steep and the train rattles at speed towards Kalávrita, beneath cliffs sculpted by erosion.

3 Kalávrita

The small town stands at the head of a fertile valley, 750m above sea level and dominated by the saw-edged peaks of the Aroánia Óri (Aroania range). At the **Monastery of Áyia Lavra**, 7km from the town, Archbishop Germanos proclaimed the revolt on 25 March 1821 which became the War of Independence. The monastery, burned by the Turks in 1821 and the Germans in 1943, houses a small museum (open 8am–1pm & 5pm–sunset). The Koimisos tis Theotokou (Cathedral of the Virgin Mary) in Kalávrita's main square was also burned by both Turks and Germans. One of its two clocks is permanently stopped at 2.34pm, the time at which 1,436 villagers were massacred by the Nazis on 13 December 1943, an event also marked by a monument above the village. History aside, Kalávrita is a pleasant, quiet village with a cool *platia* shaded by trees in front of the cathedral.

Stereá Ellás

Stereá Ellás (Sterea Ellas) is a narrow coastal strip bounded in the south by the calm waters of the Korinthiakós Kólpos (Gulf of Corinth) and dominated in the north by a series of thinly-populated mountain ranges. From east to west, these are Panaitolikón, Vardhoúsia, Gióna and Parnassós. In the northwest the Amvrakikós Kólpos (Amvrakic Gulf) takes a bite out of the coast and separates the region from neighbouring Ipiros (Epirus).

Ósios Loukás monastery has some of the finest Byzantine frescoes and mosaics in Greece

The sightseeing high point is the ancient sanctuary of Delfi (Delphi), second only to the Acropolis among the classical sites of Greece. There are medieval castles aplenty, too.

Inland, the region displays striking mountain scenery, including one of Greece's handful of ski resorts, while on the west coast the Ionian Sea laps at some of the mainland's least-visited beaches.

A major highway from Athens and Thebes passes through Levádhia (Livadhia), Arákhova and Delphi before meeting the coast at Itéa. It then skirts the Gulf of Corinth on its way to Andírrion, Mesolóngion and points north and west.

Stereá Ellás

A gold mosaic decorates a doorway at Ósios Loukás monastery

Arákhova commands the pass over Parnassós

DELPHI ROAD
Arákhova
Though its steep-roofed, half-timbered houses tremble to the passing of heavy traffic on the main highway which runs through the town, Arákhova is quite peaceful. Off the busy main street, lined with restaurants and souvenir shops selling rugs and sheepskin coats, it is pleasantly peaceful and its location – above Delphi, commanding a pass over the shoulder of 2,457m Parnassós – affords fine views in all directions. With bare hills above and below, it has a cool, almost alpine climate and Athenians come here to ski on the Parnon pistes above the town as late as April.
34km west of Levádhia.

Khairónia/Chaironeia (Heronia)
A gigantic marble lion guards the battlefield where in 338 BC the pikemen and cavalry of Macedon crushed the combined forces of the southern city-states, led by Thebes. The 5.5m statue marked the grave of the warriors of the elite Sacred Band of Thebes, who fought to the death. Greek guerrilla fighters in the War of Independence smashed it open, hoping to find treasure, but found nothing. It was pieced together some 80 years later and re-erected. The town is also the birthplace of Plutarch, the Greek historian and philosopher (c.46–c.120).
11km north of Levádhia.

Levádhia
There is no sign today of the meadows from which this unkempt but not unappealing town takes its name. In medieval times Levádhia was the most important town in the region, thanks to its strategic site controlling routes between Athens and the west and north. Although a handful of the old Turkish-style houses with overhanging upper storeys and wrought-iron balconies survive, and the dome of a derelict mosque can be spotted at the corner of Tsogka and Stratigo Ioannou, for the most part Levádhia is uncompromisingly modern.

A clear, fast-running stream springs from a source below the limestone crag on which the town's 14th-century castle stands, and is crossed near its source by a hump-backed Turkish mule bridge. It takes about 20 minutes to scramble through pine woods to the dilapidated castle, but the climb is worth it for the view of Parnassós to the west and the fertile farmlands of the eastern plain.
190km west of Athens.

Frourio (Fortress), signposted 750m from town centre. Free access.

Orkhomenós

Just outside the unassuming agricultural town of Orkhomenós are the ruins of the ancient settlement, a powerful city in Mycenaean times. The most prominent remnants are the theatre and, next to it, a collapsed Mycenaean chamber-tomb dating from the city's heyday in the 14th century BC. Climb to the top of the hill on which the acropolis of the city once stood for an extensive bird's-eye view of the ancient site.

Orkhomenós is 11km northeast of Levadhia. The ruins are 1km east of the town centre on the road to Kástron. Open: Tue–Sun 8.30am–3pm.

Ósios Loukás

The Byzantine church was completed in 1019 on the site of an earlier hermitage of St Luke the Styriote, who was celebrated for his miraculous healings and prophecies. It is built in the formal style, with a central dome over an eight-sided body. The best-preserved of the great Byzantine churches, it has 16 arched windows surrounded by mosaics of the prophets and surmounted by angels. The apse is dominated by a mosaic of the Virgin and Child. The exterior is a typical patchwork of brick and stone in the Byzantine manner.

Next to the main church is the Church of the Theotokos, where services are still held. On the gallery of the second floor of the monastic buildings opposite, note the wooden bar and metal chimes which are struck to call the monastery's handful of monks to prayer.

9km south of the main Levádhia/Itéa road, follow signs to Dhístomon, then to Ósios Loukás. Tel: (226) 702 2797. Open: daily 8am–5.30pm. Admission charge.

The monastic church of Ósios Loukás is the best-preserved of Greece's Byzantine churches

Delfí

Delphi

The centre of the Ancient Greek world, the Delphi site is the most powerfully magnetic classical site outside Athens. Much of its charisma stems from its location, carefully chosen by its founders to amplify the awed emotions of pilgrims as they approached the sanctuaries and the oracle.

Close to the mouth of a deep gorge in the side of Parnassós, Delphi is ringed by massive peaks and looks south over a delta of olive groves which flows from the foothills down to the shores of the Gulf of Corinth. The amphi-theatrical plan of the Sanctuary of Apollo is echoed by the 300m cliffs which loom above it. *The archaeological sites are separated by the main Delphi-Arákhova road.*

Ierós Dhrómos (The Sacred Way and The Main Site)

The most fully restored buildings of the main site are the porticoed Treasury of the Athenians; the votive offering of the Athenians, a Doric building erected in 490–480 BC in order to commemorate the victory of Marathón; the 4th-century BC Temple of Apollo with six of its 50-

plus Doric columns standing; the 2nd-century BC Theatre; and the 3rd-century BC Stadium. Just above the Treasury of the Athenians a very ordinary-looking boulder marks the location of the famed Oracle.

These and the founda-tions of other treasuries are connected by the Sacred Way, a broad, stepped road which zig-zags from the main entrance to the Stadium, from which there are fine views of the site and of the Temple of Athena, below the main road. *1km east of the modern village of Delphi, above the Delphi-Arákhova road. Tel: (226) 508 2312. Open: Mon–Fri 7.30am–6pm, weekends & holidays 8.30am–2.45pm. Admission charge.*

Mousío Arkheologikoú (Archaeological Museum)
One of the finest museums

THE ORACLE OF DELPHI

The earth-mother Gaia was worshipped at Delphi from the 14th century BC through priestesses who were intoxicated by fumes rising from fissures in the earth. With the advent of the Dorians, Gaia was supplanted by Apollo and the site became his greatest sanctuary. Apollo's mouthpiece was the Sybil or Pythia, whose tranced utterings in answer to pilgrims' questions were translated into verse by her priests. The answers, ambiguous as they were, were not forecasts but advice.

in Greece, containing fragments of friezes, *kouroi*, bronzes of griffons and sphinxes, ivory figurines and heads of Artemis and Apollo, and a splendid lifesize statue of a bull in silver and gold. Top billing goes to the Bronze Charioteer, the masterpiece of an unknown artist of around 478 BC. The site was excavated by French archaeologists, and most of the museum labelling is in French and Greek. *Signposted, 100m west of entrance to main archaeological site. Tel: (226) 508 2175. Open: daily 9am–3pm. Admission charge includes both site and museum.*

Tholos (Rotunda)

Below the Sanctuary of Apollo stood two temples of Athena, a 6th-century BC Doric building which was abandoned in the 4th century BC and replaced by a newer, smaller temple. Only the foundations of these remain. Between the sites of the two temples stand the three surviving columns of one of Delphi's most fully reconstructed relics, the Tholos. This circular 4th-century building was probably a shrine to Gaia. *500m east of main archaeological site, below the Delphi-Arákhova road. Tel & opening hours as for main site. Admission charge*

Vrísi Kastalías (Kastalian Spring)

The sacred spring, a mere trickle of water for most of the year, emerges from a narrow gorge between the two cliffs which dominate the site of the Sanctuary. Here, pilgrims washed themselves before entering the Sanctuary. Two stone basins used for this ritual can be seen carved in the base of the cliff. *100m east of the entrance to the Sanctuary of Apollo. Closed for stabilisation of rocks.*

The treasury of the Athenians at Delphi

Aphrodite

Born from the sea, Aphrodite was the goddess of love and beauty. Her most important temple on the mainland was at Corinth.

Apollo

Apollo was the god of male beauty and patron of the fine arts.
His greatest sanctuary was at Delphi, but he was also worshipped at Corinth and Vassai (Vassae).

Ares

The god of war and lover of Aphrodite.

Artemis

Twin sister of Apollo, Artemis the huntress is the goddess of chastity. Vravróna and Delphi were her most important temples.

Asklepios

The god of healing and son of Apollo. His major shrine was at Epídhavros.

Athena

The patron goddess of Athens had many aspects. She was the deity of wisdom, arts and crafts, and of victory. Her greatest temple was the Parthenon.

Demeter

Goddess of fertility, worshipped principally at Elevsís.

Dionysos

The god of wine, joy and revelry, worshipped in Athens and on Mount Parnassós.

Hades

The king of the dead, whose oracle was the Nekromantion at Efira (Efyra).

Helios

The sun-god. Many of the tiny mountain chapels of Áyios Ilias (the prophet Elijah) may once have been his temples, an interesting play on the similarly-pronounced names.

Hephaistos

God of fire and metal, hence of smiths, and husband of Aphrodite. Worshipped at his principal temple, now called the Thission, in Athens.

Hera

Hera was the wife of Zeus, greatest of the gods, and is the goddess of marriage. Her main temples were at Árgos and Olympia.

Hermes

The messenger of the gods, and so the god of commerce, communication and eloquence.

Hestia

Hestia was the goddess of hearth and home.

Leto

A minor goddess, lover of Zeus and mother of Apollo and Artemis.

Persephone

The daughter of Demeter and wife of Hades, Persephone was the goddess of death and renewal. Worshipped with her husband at the Nekromantion.

Poseidon

The god of the sea, storms and earthquakes, second only to his brother Zeus, Poseidon's main shrines were at Athens and Cape Soúnion.

Zeus

King of the gods and ruler of the world, Zeus was worshipped principally at Olympia and Dhodhóni (Dodoni).

Facing page above: head of Asklepios in the British Museum; below: the god Poseidon protects a Greek *tavérna*
Above: frieze depicting the marriage of Hebe and Herakles

THE GULF OF CORINTH
Ámfissa

A small medieval castle, the stronghold of the Catalan mercenaries who dominated this part of Greece in the 13th century AD, overlooks Ámfissa, on the shore of the 'sea of olives' which covers the plain below Delphi. North of the plain, the sharp-peaked 2,510m Gióna (Gionia) massif rises steeply. There are quaint 18th-century streets around the old *platia*, overlooked by the pine-clad castle peak.
8km northwest of Delphi.

Andírrion

A squat Venetian fortress guards the busy pier of this port on the narrowest part of the Gulf of Corinth. On the south shore of the gulf, its twin guards the pretty harbour of Rion.
12km west of Navpaktos. Ferries run at 15–30 minute intervals between the two, linking Patras and the Peloponnese with the northern mainland.

Galaxídhion

Galaxídhion is one of the gems of the Gulf coast, a charming town on a headland between two sheltered bays. Tall 19th-century mansions, fishing boats and seafood restaurants crowd the waterfront below a huddle of pretty balconied houses rising to the dome of a grand 19th-century church built by one of the town's many prosperous ship-owners, all reflected in the mirror of the double harbour. If Galaxídhion had a beach it would be perfect; even without one

THE BATTLE OF LEPANTO

On 7 October 1571 a Turkish fleet of 200 galleys commanded by Ali Pasha sailed from Návpaktos – then called Lepanto – to do battle with the fleet of the Holy League, an alliance of Venetian, Spanish, Genoese, Neapolitan and Papal forces. These had been called together by the Pope to defend Christendom from Turkey's westward surge. The fleet was commanded by Don John of Austria, bastard son of the Holy Roman Emperor Charles V.

Among the Christian combatants were Miguel de Cervantes (1547–1616), author of *Don Quixote*, who lost the use of his left hand in the battle, and the Genoese commander Giovanni Andrea Dorea. Although outnumbered by the Turkish galleys, Don John's fleet shattered the myth of Ottoman invincibility by destroying 200 Turkish ships while losing 10 of his own, and halted Turkish expansion westward for a generation.

The town of Galaxídhion prospered in the 19th century

The extensive Venetian harbour fortifications of Návpaktos

it is one of the pleasantest stops on this coast.

25km southwest of Delphi.

Itéa

Itéa offers the only beaches of any kind for around 30km in either direction, with a short crescent of pebbles at the east end of its eucalyptus-lined esplanade and a second stretch of grey sand and pebble beach just around the corner. Otherwise, Itéa fails to live up to the inspiring backdrop of Parnassós and Gionia behind it and the peaks of Killíni across the Gulf.

12km south of Delphi.

Návpaktos

Battlements and turrets surround the holiday-postcard harbour of this little port and scramble up through the town centre to enclose a substantial 15th-century Venetian castle among pine trees on the hill above.

Behind the harbour, a huge flagstoned square is shaded by pines and plane trees and cluttered with café tables. A busy modern town stretches either side of the old-fashioned centre.

160km west of Levádhia.

The Catalan Company

Ámfissa was a stronghold of the Catalan Company, a force of mercenary soldiers from Spain, who set out alongside the knights of the Fourth Crusade in 1204. When the crusaders sacked Constantinople in 1204 the Catalans gained the region between Ámfissa and Levádhia, where they built castles. They were vassals of the Frankish dukes of Athens, but they turned on Duke Gautier de Brienne and on 13 March 1311 at the battle of Kifissos, near Orkhomenós, the Catalan infantry defeated his 700 knights by luring them into marshy ground. The Catalan Company vanished from history soon after with the recovery of the Byzantine Empire in Greece in the 14th and 15th centuries.

THE WESTERN STEREA
Akhelóös

The Akhelóös River, one of Greece's largest, meets the Ionian Sea in a wide fertile delta whose vast expanse of channels and reedbeds is gradually giving way to maize and cotton fields. The delta is a haven for waterbirds. Kingfishers streak along the riverbanks, egrets stalk among the salt-pans and fish traps lining the marshy shore, and storks nest in treetops and on the chimneys and telephone poles of local villages. The delta, a paradise for birdwatchers, is threatened by encroaching cultivation and by plans for further damming of the Akhelóös, whose northern reaches are already blocked by hydro-electric dams.
Access by dirt roads west of Katokhí, 21km from Mesolóngion, where the river's mighty main channel is crossed by the main Mesolóngion–Astakós road.

Astakós

Looking west to the island of Itháki (Ithaca), this tranquil harbour at the end of a long, narrow inlet dotted with desert islands offers little excitement, though a colourful sunset can be enjoyed from the comfort of a café seat on its *tavérna*-lined esplanade.
50km northwest of Mesolóngion.

Mesolóngion (Missolonghi)

Missolonghi's famous lagoon, a patchwork of fish farms and salt pans, is spectacular when seen from the causeway which links the mainland town with its island suburb of Tourlida, a haphazard collection of fishing shacks with a handful of summer-only fish *tavérnas*. The historic town itself was much damaged in World War II.
35km west of Andírrion.

Píli Exodhoú (Gate of the Exodus)

Passing through what remains of the city walls, the gate is famed for the sortie made by 9,000 defenders of the city, women and children, in a desperate attempt to escape their Turkish besiegers in April 1826, during the War of Independence. They were betrayed, and fewer than 2,000 escaped to Ámfissa, 80km away. The last defenders blew up their powder magazine to

BYRON AT MISSOLONGHI

The Romantic poet George Gordon, Lord Byron (1788–1824), is remembered all over Greece in squares and street names, his name Hellenicized as Vironos. Always an admirer of Greece and an enthusiastic supporter of Greek independence, he landed at Missolonghi in January 1824 determined to fight for the Greek cause and was elected its commander-in-chief. Before his complete lack of military experience could do any damage, however, he died in April of fever. Ironically, his untimely death helped to rally European opinion behind the Greek struggle. He probably did Greece more good as a dead hero than as a live commander.

take as many of their attackers with them as possible.
Signposted.

Iroon Kipos (Park of the Heroes)

Next to the Gate of the Exodus, with modern statues of Byron and the Greek leader Markos Botzaris and other heroes of the 1821–30 war.

Mítikas

So many islands dot the Ionian Sea off Mítikas that this undiscovered one-street village with its 3km sweep of white pebble beach seems to be on a landlocked lake. Kalamos, the biggest of them, is only 500m offshore and a small ferry plies between the village and the

handful of houses on the pine-covered island, where the battlements of a tiny 16th-century fortress overlook the bay.
84km northwest of Mesolóngion.

Vónitsa

A huge castle squats above the silvery waters of the Amvrakic Gulf, overlooking the naturally sheltered harbour and esplanade at Vónitsa, a clutter of two- and three-storey Italianate houses and a stretch of pebbly beach. The 16th-century fortress was built by the Venetians to control the passage into the Gulf, an enormous mirror-like lagoon dotted with uninhabited islets.
120km northwest of Mesolóngion.

The Akhelóös River meets the sea in a vast spread of channels and reedbeds

Tour: Arákhova, Delphi, Ámfissa and Galaxídhion

This tour takes in a cross-section of countryside from the pretty mountain village of Arákhova on the slopes of Parnassós to Galaxídhion on its bay of islands.

Allow 5 hours.

1 Arákhova

Perched on the shoulder of the 2,457-m high Mount Parnassós at a height of 900m, Arákhova has great views and in winter is popular with skiers visiting the mountain's pistes. In summer it is pleasantly cool.

For 10km west of Arákhova the road snakes

down the north side of a deep valley with olive terraces below and bare mountain slopes above. After 8km you will get your first glimpse of the Gulf of Corinth ahead, and after a further 1km the columns of the Temple of Apollo at Delphi come into sight. Allow at least 3 hours for Delphi's sites and museums (see pp88–9).

2 Delphi

Modern Delphi exists solely to service visitors to the ancient sanctuary. Its two parallel main streets are packed with hotels and uniformly mediocre restaurants.

The road hairpins down towards the sea until, 5km below Delphi, it passes beneath itself in a tight loop and bridge. Follow signs for Itéa and Ámfissa. After 5km you reach the fringes of the 'sea of olives' and continue for 10km through the groves to Ámfissa.

3 Ámfissa

This unassuming little town is crowned by a pretty 13th-century castle among pines on a crag. Built by Franks and Catalan mercenaries, it incorporates remnants of the earlier classical acropolis. The walls surround the remains of a keep, round tower, chapel and barracks.

Leave the town by Odos Ethniki Antistasi, which runs from the south side of Ámfissa's main square, and climb in zigzags for 5km, leaving the olive-groves behind, and emerge suddenly on bare hillside with the rocky peak of Gionia on the northern skyline. The road skirts the flank of the Gionia massif, trending south towards the Gulf of Corinth.

4 Áyia Evthímia (Áyia Ethimia)

Set among fields and almond trees, Áyia Ethimia is an attractive old-fashioned village of red-tiled stone houses. This part of the drive is especially pretty in spring, when the fields are vivid with wild flowers, and in autumn, when the almond orchards turn a brilliant red.

5 Vouníkhora (Vounihora)

The village is surrounded by a distinctive maze of grey dry-stone sheepfold walls. The road now climbs steeply over barren slopes with fine views to the north and of Parnassós with Delphi and Arákhova perched on its flanks to the east.

The whole Gulf of Corinth panorama comes into view 2km beyond Vouníkhora and after a further 3km you turn left, following signs to Pendéoria and Galaxídhion in a series of hairpins until you meet the main coast road 1km east of Galaxídhion. The turn-off to the village is on the inland side of the highway and passes beneath the main road.

6 Galaxídhion

A substantial domed church, built in the last century by one of Galaxídhion's wealthy shipowners, surmounts this pretty village on a headland at the mouth of the Kólpos Itéas (Gulf of Itéa). With its double harbour, fishing boats, yachts, fish restaurants and waterfront dominated by tall, elegant 19th-century houses, Galaxídhion seems to belong more to the islands than the mainland. It lacks only a beach to make it perfect.

Wealthy shipowners' mansions from Galaxídhion's 19th-century heyday

Ípiros and Thessalía

Epirus and Thessaly

The two regions which make up the central part of the northern mainland could hardly be more different. In the west, the Píndhos mountains which form the spine of Epirus conceal some of the wildest and most beautiful country in Europe, sheltering Greece's last remaining bears, wolves, griffon vultures and other endangered species. The Píndhos's eastern slopes descend steeply to the rolling farmlands of Thessaly, the richest agricultural land in Greece.

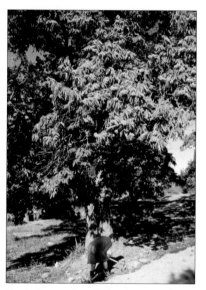

Chestnuts are an important cash crop on the Pelion peninsula

These are regions of climatic extremes, too. The Píndhos summits, reaching heights of more than 2,600m, are snowbound for up to five months, while Europe's highest summer temperatures have been recorded on the plains of Thessaly.

Some of Greece's most picturesque mountain villages are to be found in the Zagória region of Epirus and on the Pelion peninsula of Thessaly.

Other highlights of central Greece include the old-fashioned towns of Ioánnina and Metsovo and the cliff-top monasteries of the Metéora, and in contrast, there are fine beaches on both Epirus's Ionian coast and Thessaly's Aegean shores.

Epirus and Thessaly

The Píndhos mountain range

CENTRAL THESSALY
Kalabáka (Kalambaka)

As you approach Kalambaka, the gentle contours and agricultural patchwork of the Thessalian lowlands start to rise towards the grand highlands of the Píndhos range. Behind the unexciting market town, a blank 555-m cliff face rises, a landmark to show you are approaching the unearthly landscape of the Metéora.

21km north of Trikkala.

Metéora

Nothing prepares you for the scenic impact of this valley lined with soaring towers of rock, each crowned by a precarious monastery. The views over Thessaly and the valley of the upper Piniós are breathtaking. Only six of two dozen monasteries dating from the 14th century are open, and only five are inhabited, some of them by a solitary monk or nun. Two – Áyia Triadha and Áyios Stefanos – are functioning monastic houses, while the rest are preserved as religious museums.

Áyios Nikólaos (Saint Nicholas)

Áyios Nikolaos is a recently-restored 14th-century monastery whose 16th-century chapel is decorated with frescoes of the Last Judgement by the Cretan painter Theophanes. They are all the more striking for their restoration.
Closed: in winter.

Áyios Stéphanos (Saint Stephen)

Now a nunnery, Áyios Stéphanos was founded in the 14th century and has two churches, a 14th-century basilica with frescoes and a later 18th-century building. The museum houses manuscripts, embroideries and some striking icons.
Closed: Mon.

Áyia Triádha (Holy Trinity)

The 15th-century monastery may look familiar; the James Bond epic *For Your Eyes Only* (1981) was shot here. The building sits atop one of the tallest of the natural pillars.
Closed: Thu.

Méga Metéoron (Great Meteoron)

This is the grandest and most venerable of the monasteries, with a small museum in its 16th-century refectory and well-preserved frescoes in the dome of its 15th–16th-century church.
Closed: Tue.

Ósios Varlaám

Ósios Varlaám also has a frescoed chapel and the prettiest flower-gardens of all the monasteries. Here, too, you can see the perilous-looking winch used in the past to haul up monks and visitors as well as supplies. Its church of Áyioi Pandes (All Saints) dates from the 16th century and has perhaps the finest frescoes of all the monastery churches, including scenes of the Last Judgement and the life of St John the Baptist.
Closed: Fri.

Roussánou

The monastery of Roussanou, with its red-tiled roof, is dizzyingly located on a crag which looks ready to topple away from the cliff face and is reached by a vertigo-inducing footbridge.
Closed: Wed.

The valley of the Metéora begins at Kastraki, 3km from Kalambaka. The trip, taking in all six monasteries, is 17km. For all monasteries tel: (243) 202 2278. Open: 9am–1pm & 3.30–6pm; hours vary from monastery to monastery, sometimes closed on holy days & religious festivals. Admission charge for each monastery. Dress code: long trousers for men, skirts below the knee for women, long sleeves for both. Women wearing trousers are provided with an over-shirt at the entrance.

Métsovon (Metsovo)

Local costume – typified by the clog-like shoes with red woollen pom-poms on sale in every souvenir shop – is dying out slowly, and you are most likely to see it worn on feast days. At 1,000m above sea level, Metsovo is bitterly cold in winter, so the colourful rugs and blankets which brighten Metsovo's main-street shops are no surprise. The view eastward over the fertile farmlands of Thessaly contrasts sharply with the hostile peaks of the Píndhos to the west. Above the town, the highest pass in Greece (1,705m) carries the main road between Thessaly and Epirus.

90km nortrhwest of Trikkala.

Arkhondikó Tositsa (Tositsa Mansion)

The restored 18th-century mansion was the home of the wealthy Tositsa family, native philanthropists, who also endowed the nearby Idhrima Tositsa (Tositsa Foundation).

Its exhibition includes traditional costumes and textiles.

On the main street. Open: daily except Thu, 8.30am–1pm & 4–6pm. Admission charge.

Tríkkala

A dusty market town with a thriving old-fashioned bazaar area left over from its heyday as capital of the region under Turkish rule, Tríkkala stands on a low hill crowned by a crumbling Byzantine castle and is surrounded by farms.

61km west of Larisa.

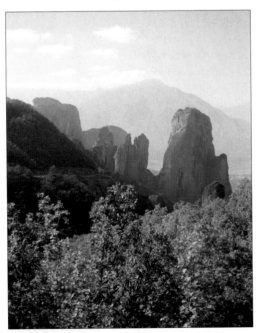

The rocky pillars and pinnacles of the Metéora, which means, appropriately, 'in the air'

The Greek Orthodox Church moved away from the Western Catholic Church over several centuries, the final split coming in 1074 when the Pope and the Patriarch in Constantinople excommunicated each other. Under the Ottoman Empire, Greece was cut off from the Christian West and the split became permanent. Clerics like Archbishop Germanos of Patras, who declared the start of the War of Independence in 1821, were often in the forefront during the many rebellions against the Turks.

The village priest with his black robe, stovepipe hat and beard is one of the chief characters of any Greek community. Most Greeks feel that to be Greek is to be Orthodox, and the Church helped to keep the flame of Greek language and culture alight during the long centuries of Turkish rule. It is still very much a living religion, and Greece sometimes seems to have more churches than it needs. Even a small village may have two or three churches and chapels – Greeks who were successful overseas or in business have traditionally thanked their patron saint by building a church or chapel in his or her name.

Oddly enough, the head (the Patriarch) of the Greek Orthodox Church lives not in Athens but in Istanbul (still called Constantinopolis by Greeks), the last living relic of the great Christian empire of Byzantium. Monks and abbots rank higher in the hierarchy of the Orthodox Church than priests and bishops, but married men may become priests – all those Greek names beginning with 'Papa' indicate a priest roosting somewhere in the family tree.

Sacred relics and centuries-old icons are a vital part of

the Orthodox faith and are said to have miraculous powers. No church or chapel, however remote, is ever without its complement of flickering candles, kept alight by the devout.

The Church comes into its own at Easter, the biggest festival of the Greek year, when holy icons are paraded through the streets and solemn services are held by censer-swinging bishops draped in sumptuous silken robes.

Long robes and beards typify the village priest, ornately dressed for festivals
Above right: icons represent the richness and colour of Byzantine art

ICONS

The finest of Greece's ancient icons have an impact as strong as anything by Picasso. Icons – paintings of Christ, the Virgin, saints or angels – are Greece's direct link with the great Byzantine empire in its heyday. Some are more than 1,000 years old, but for sheer beauty there is nothing to choose between these and icons painted as late as the 18th and 19th centuries. The style is strict, and the purpose is always to lift the spirit. Authentic icons are virtually impossible to buy, and taking them out of the country is against the law, but several modern icon artists such as Kostas Georgopoulos paint wonderful replicas which are faithful to the original. Georgopoulos uses up to 30 different materials, from silver and gold leaf to natural dyes mixed with egg yolk, animal glues, old hewn boards, and 10 different ageing chemicals.

IOÁNNINA AND AROUND
Dhodhóni (Dodona)

The oldest sacred site on the Greek mainland stands in a remote valley among fields and sees few visitors. Dedicated to the Great Goddess from 2000 BC before becoming a sanctuary of Zeus from around 1300 BC, the most impressive feature is the theatre. Massive walls and column stumps outline the Temple of Herakles and the Sanctuary of Zeus.

21km southwest of Ioánnina, signposted 13km west of the main Ioánnina-Árta road. Tel: (265) 108 2287.
Open: weekdays 8am–7pm (till 5pm in winter), weekends & holidays 8.30am–3pm. Admission charge.

Ioánnina

Ioánnina's location on pea-green Limni Pamvotis/Límni Ioánninon (Lake Pamvotis), surrounded by rugged peaks, cannot be bettered. A tumbledown bazaar area, a 1,300-year-old walled town, and a handful of mosques and minarets surviving from Turkish times give the town an oriental air.

469km northwest of Athens.

Mousío Arkheologikoú (Archaeological Museum)

A well-displayed collection of bronze tools and weapons, stone and bone implements, and finds from Dhodhóni.

Platia 25 Martiou. Tel: (265) 103 3357.
Open: Tue–Sun 8.30am–3pm. Admission charge.

Froúrion (Fortress)

The fortress town is ringed by walls built in AD 528 by the Emperor Justinian against the rampaging Goths. A tree-lined esplanade runs along the lake front. Enter the walls by the Glikidhon gate, off Dionysou Filosofotou just south of the café-filled square below the northeast bastion. Within, a derelict Turkish barracks stands beside a dusty parade-ground.

Dimotikoú Mousío (Popular Museum)

Rusting cannon and a pyramid of cannon-balls greet you as you enter the former mosque of Aslan Pasha. Some of the cannon bear the lion crest of the Republic of Venice or the double eagle of the Russian Tsars. There is a fine view of Pamvotis from the square outside the museum. Built in 1618 on the site of a church of St John the Baptist, the mosque was in use until 1922 and became a museum in 1933. Displays include relics and costumes of Ioánnina's Greek, Turkish and Jewish communities.

Alexiou Noutsou. Signposted from the entrance to the fortress. Open: daily 8.30am–3pm. Admission charge.

Mousío Laografías (Museum of Folklore)

Silver jewellery, chased brass trays and Sarakatsan embroidery and weaving are displayed with folk costumes in an old mansion with vividly painted ceilings.

Mihail Angelou 42. Tel: (265) 102 3566.
Open: Mon–Fri 9am–2pm, Sat–Sun 10am–3.30pm. Admission charge.

Museum of Greek History

The work of one man, Pavlos Vrellis, this new museum is one of the most popular in Greece. Vrellis bought the

17-acre rocky land in 1983 when he was a 60-year-old pensioner, designed it in the form of an urban sentry's box in Epirus in the 18th century and worked singlehandedly to create the 36 exhibits as exact replicas of figures and events from the 17th century until 1982.
12th km, Ioannina-Athens Rd, Bizani Ioannina. Tel/fax: (065 109 2128. Open: daily, Apr–Sep 9.30am–5pm; Oct–Mar 10am–4pm.

Tsámi Fethye (Victory Mosque)

The derelict mosque built in 1430, stands amid ruins in a fortress within a fortress.
Overlooking Platia Katsandoni. Closed to the public.

Nissí (Island)

Glass tanks full of live carp, eels, crayfish and crabs greet visitors to Lake Pamvotis's only island, a favourite trip for diners from Ioánnina. Some restaurateurs keep turtles, salamanders and even baby alligators – not to eat, but to catch your eye.

Five monasteries, the oldest dating from the 11th century and the most recent from the 17th, are dotted around the island.
Boats go to the island from Ioánnina every half hour (hourly in winter) from the pier on Dionysou Filosofotou, close to the northeast corner of the fortress.

Moní Áyios Padeleímonas (Monastery of St Panteleimon)

Small exhibition of books and archives.

Mousío Alí-Pashá (Ali Pasha Museum)

Within the monastery walls, in what were the monks' cells, a museum of etchings, watercolours and antiques commemorates Ali Pasha, the Albanian warlord who ruled Epirus from 1788 until he was shot in 1822 for rebelling against the Sultan. You can still see the bullet-holes in the floor.
Platia Monaxon Nektario-Theofanos. Signposted from the waterfront. Open: daily 8am–8pm. Admission charge to Ali Pasha museum only.

Pérama Spiliá/Spilaion Peramatos (Perama Caves)

Greece's largest cave system, accidentally discovered in 1940, extends for 2km into the hillside, winding through grottoes full of twisted spikes and spires.
In the centre of Perama village, 5km northwest of Ioánnina. Tel: (265) 108 521. Open: daily 8am–8pm (till 4pm in winter). Admission charge.

Fishing boats moored at the mouth of the Akherónda

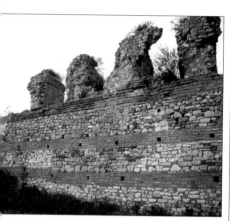

Roman ramparts at the lost city of Nikópolis, abandoned in AD 1040

THE EPIRUS COAST
Akherónda (Acheron River)

A strong-flowing icy stream, the Acheron emerges from a fissure in the mountainside, 4km inland from the hamlet of Glyki. It reaches the sea as a wide, turquoise river at Amoudia, where it has created a 500-m sandy beach, behind which is a broad delta of fields and reedbeds.

3km west of the main coast road.

Amvrakikós Kólpos (Amvrakic Gulf)

A huge, silvery lagoon dotted with uninhabited islands separates Epirus from Sterea Ellas. Shuttle ferries cross its 750-m wide mouth between Préveza and the southern shore. Off the northern cape on which Préveza stands, Octavian and Mark Anthony fought the sea-battle of Aktion (Actium) in 31 BC (see Nikópolis). The north shore, between Préveza and Menídhi, is a region of salt-marshes and brackish lagoons which attract migrating birds, but has nothing to offer non-birdwatchers.

Árta

Árta was an important town in Roman and medieval times. Little remains of its former glory except a celebrated 18th-century Turkish bridge across the Arakhthos River, currently being restored. The 13th-century walls incorporate fragments of earlier classical and Hellenistic buildings.

75km south of Ioánnina.

Efira Nekromantion (Necromanteion of Efyra)

In ancient times the Acheron, also known as the Styx, was thought to flow from the underworld and an Oracle of the Dead stood on what was then an island and is now a low hill surrounded by fields. Pilgrims passed through a labyrinth of corridors to question the priestess, who had to be at least 50 years old.

Offerings to Hades and Persephone were lowered into a shrine below, believed to be the upper part of Hades' underground palace. A wall of giant blocks surrounds the site, where a small Byzantine church with frescoes of the Virgin and saints stands above the chamber of the oracle.

Signposted 1km from Amoudia on the main coast roads. Tel: (268) 104 1026. Open: daily 8.30am–3pm.

Igoumenítsa

A seaport close to the Albanian border, Igoumenítsa is the ideal place to catch a ferry to Corfu or Italy.

101km west of Ioánnina.

Nikópolis

Scattered over a vast area, brick and stone walls, gateways and the arches of an aqueduct rise from the woods and fields. Two small archaeological sites are enclosed, but the most impressive part of Nikópolis and the best place from which to view the whole site is the theatre, accessible at any time. The stadium, opposite the theatre, is over-grown and indistinguishable to any but the most experienced eye. The site is powerfully evocative of lost glories. Built by Octavian, the future Roman Emperor Augustus, to mark his victory over Mark Anthony and Cleopatra at Aktion (31 BC), the city was abandoned in 1040 after being sacked by the Bulgars.

8km north of Preveza.
Archaeological site, signposted. Tel: (268)
204 1336. Open: daily, summer
8.30am–5pm; winter 8.30am–3pm.
Admission charge.

Párga

Once a Venetian harbour, Párga is a lively holiday resort. Rows of brightly painted houses climb from a crescent bay dotted with islands to a hill crowned by a Venetian castle. North of this headland stretches a 1-km sandy beach. There are smaller beaches either side of the headland at the south end of the bay, and others can be reached by motorboats which run frequently throughout the day in summer.

50km north of Préveza.

Kástro (Castle)

The walls surround an inner ring of battlements and a 13th-century keep, where rusting cannon lie scattered.

Open: daily 8am–8pm (till 5pm in winter). Free admission.

Préveza

There are adequate beaches a few kilometres northwest of town, but Préveza offers little else to the holidaymaker. The main road turns inland towards Párga, and shuttle ferries cross the mouth of the Amvrakic Gulf to the Sterea Ellas shore.

125km south of Ioánnina.

Rocky islands punctuate the bay in front of the whitewashed buildings of Párga

LÁRISA, ÓSSA AND THE VALE OF TEMPE

Lárisa

A town of few charms, Lárisa's importance as a road junction in medieval times is reflected by a frowning medieval castle on a central hilltop over-looking the Piniós River, which flows through the town. Lárisa stood guard over routes north, south, east and west. Today, it is bypassed by National Road 1, which turns northeast from the city to enter the Vale of Tempe.
318km north of Athens.

Óssa

Like a mountain in a child's story, Óssa stands alone, its often cloud-capped peak rising sharply from the cotton fields of the Thessalian plain. Rising to 1,978m, Óssa is dwarfed by its giant neighbour, the 2,917m Ólimbos (Olympus) not far to the north.

A logging road, more suitable for four-wheel-drive vehicles than for saloon cars, runs from the hill hamlet of Spili over the shoulder of the mountain to the sea, with vertiginous views of misty canyons, forest slopes and the Olympus massif.

The Greek Alpine Society (EOS) maintains a mountain shelter closer to the summit for those who want to trek to the top of the peak.

Stómion

Stómion is a quiet harbour-cum-resort close to the mouth of the Piniós River, where lagoons, channels and reed-beds shelter storks, kingfishers, herons and other waterbirds. A sandy, deserted beach runs north. The green slopes of Óssa to the south and the cloud-capped Olympus to the north make a breathtaking backdrop.
40km northeast of Larisa.

Vale of Tempe

The Piniós River flows from its source in the Píndhos mountains across the plain of Thessaly before passing through the once-romantic Vale. Here, legend says, the nymph Daphne was changed to a laurel tree to save here from Apollo's amorous advances. The deep, 12km gorge in classical times formed a natural barrier between the Greece of the southern city-states and the wilder, less civilized lands of the northern Hellenes. It now carries

The Vale of Tempe, a strategic pass since the dawn of time

GODS v GIANTS

While Zeus and the other Olympians were still consolidating their hold on the world after overthrowing Cronus and the other Titans, they faced a revolt by the serpent-footed Giants, brothers of the Titans. Led by Alcyoneus, the 24 giants tried to assault Olympus, the home of the gods, by placing Mount Pelion on Mount Óssa to make a stairway, but were defeated thanks to Heracles, who slew their leader, and Athene, who showed the Olympians a magic herb which made them invulnerable.

National Road 1 as well as the main Athens–Thessa-loníki rail line and is marred by fumes and noise. Prominently signposted, the Spring of Aphrodite and the Spring of Dafni, which flow into the Piniós, have been reduced to smelly culverts.

Ayía Paraskeví

Midway along the Vale of Tempe, a large lay-by offers the chance to pull off the road and view the Piniós River, crossed here by a suspension bridge. A better view of the river and valley is offered by small motor cruisers operating half-hour, 4km cruises on the river, departing when full (about every 30 minutes).
On OE1 (National Road 1), 4km south of the tollbooth at the north end of the Vale of Tempe.

Kástro Platamónas
(Platamon Castle)

The fortress, founded in 1204 by Boniface de Montferrat, Duke of Thessaloníki, was added to by the Byzantines in the 14th and 15th centuries and later by the Turks. Squatting close to the mouth of the Vale of Tempe, it guards the strategic route between northern and southern Greece. The walls are some 7m high, with round bastions at each corner. The octagonal inner keep is being restored and is used for performances during the annual Olympus Festival.
East of the main road on a hilltop opposite the modern village of Nea Pandeleimonas.
Open: Tue–Sun 8.30am–3pm.
Admission charge.

The Piniós River passes through the Vale of Tempe

THE NORTHERN PÍNDHOS

Drakolimin

Close to the 2,000m contour, a clear tarn at the lip of a 500m sheer drop is the home of thousands of brightly coloured newts and fire-bellied toads. It is a stiff 8-hour round trip from Mikro Pápingo, calling for above-average fitness and good boots, but well worth it.

5km east and 800m above Mikro Pápingo.

Fáranx Víkos (Vikos Gorge)

The plunge into the 13-km long, 1-km deep gorge cut by the Voïdhomátis River is one of the most dramatic – and demanding – hikes in Greece. The walk takes a full day and is only for the very fit, as you must scramble over boulders and up steep zigzag paths.

In late spring, the gorge may be inaccessible as melting snow turns the Voïdhomátis into an ice-cold torrent.

The gorge runs northwest from Monodhendhri to Megalo Pápingo.

Kalpákion

Polemikó Mousío Kalpáki (Kalpáki War Museum)

The museum's motley collection of elderly rifles, machine-guns, uniforms and other militaria commemorates Greece's against-all-odds victory over the Italian invaders here in the winter of 1940. Opposite the museum is a monument to General Ioannis Metaxas.

On the east side of the main north-south highway, 500m south of Kalpakion village, 35km north of Ioánnina. Open: daily 8am–5pm. Free admission.

Kónitsa

Bypassed by the main north–south highway, Kónitsa is a quiet, tree-filled, 19th-century town at the upper end of the vast valley of the Aóös River. Above it tower the peaks of Smólikas, Greece's second-highest mountain at 2,637m, and the Tímfi massif, rising to 2,497m at its highest.

64km north of Ioánnina.

Monodhéndhri

The stern grey limestone walls and stone-flagged roofs of Monodhéndhri perch on the very lip of the Vikos Gorge. If you do not feel up to walking the full length of the gorge, you can make the tiring but scenic descent to the river

THE ZAGÓRIA

The lovely, dramatically sited villages of this mountain region are built and roofed with the same grey stone and seem to grow from the mountains which surround them. Zagória offers the best mountain trekking in Greece, with high ranges separated by deep canyons which are dry in summer but rushing torrents as the winter snow melts. Under Turkish rule, the Zagória villages won certain tax privileges, and many local men went abroad to work, sending money home to build the handsome houses and churches which adorn the mountainsides. Many of the 40-plus villages are deserted, but tourism (a newcomer to the region) is helping to bring them back to life.

bed and back to Monodhéndhri in half a day. Several of the village's solidly-built traditional homes have been turned into comfortable guest-houses as part of the Greek National Tourist Office's traditional settlements programme. *45km northeast of Ioánnina.*

Pápingo (Megalo and Mikro)

The twin villages of Megalo (Big) and Mikro (Little) Pápingo stand at the northwest end of the Vikos Gorge, dwarfed by the enormous, pitted crags of the Tímfi massif. In the saddle, 500m above the upper village of Mikro Pápingo, you can see silhouetted the Astraka mountain refuge, a tiring three-hour walk up very steep paths. Megalo Pápingo is the most popular base for hiking and exploring in the Zagória. *51km northeast of Ioánnina.*

Ochi Day

On 28 October 1940 the Italian ambassador presented General Ioannis Metaxas, then military dictator of Greece, with an ultimatum: allow Italian troops to move through Greece to attack the British in Egypt. Metaxas is said to have answered with one word, 'Ochi' (No), and 28 October, a national holiday, is still known as Ochi Day. The Italians invaded immediately, but were turned back by the outgunned but determined Greeks, who delayed an invasion until the arrival of the German forces in April 1941.

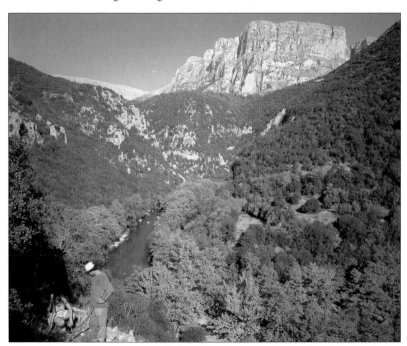

The Vikos Gorge; agility and a head for heights are essential requirements for the gorge trail

VÓLOS AND PÍLION (PELION)

The northern part of the mountainous, boot-shaped Pílion (Pelion) peninsula is watered by many streams and wooded with beech, oak and chestnut and with pear and apple orchards. The toe of the boot is barren and rugged. Pelion is separated from mainland Thessaly by the **Pagasitikós Kólpos** (Pagasitic Gulf), which laps at sheltered beaches on the west coast of the peninsula. Lush forest covers the slopes of the east coast, which drop steeply to deep blue water and white pebble beaches. Pelion's substantial half-timbered mansions with their slate roofs and elaborate polished wood interiors are among the most beautiful village homes in Greece. Many have been restored thanks to the Greek National Tourist Office's traditional settlements programme (*see p177*).

Áyios Ioánnis

A relaxed resort with a sweep of steeply shelving, east-facing sand and pebble beach below lush, tropical-looking slopes, Áyios Ioánnis is popular with Greek vacationers.
41km east of Vólos.

Makrinítsa

The most accessible of Pelion's villages, Makrinítsa is also the most affected by tourism. Many traditional homes have been converted into guest-houses. The village stands above a deep valley, its eastern slopes greenly wooded but the western side, only a few hundred metres away, dry and bare.

An arcaded church of Áyios Ioánnis Prodhromos (St John the Baptist) stands in a main square sheltered by three enormous plane trees. The urban smear of Vólos, 14km away, dominates the westward view.
14km northwest of Vólos.

Milíes/Mileai (Milies)

The frescoed church of Áyios Michaelis o Taxiarchis (St Michael 'the brigadier') stands beside an expansive balconied square with breathtaking views over the green hills of Pelion and across the silver Pagasitic Gulf. Inside the church are apocalyptic murals of saints, angels, sinners and devils. Below the square a derelict railway station awaits the restoration of the Pelion narrow-gauge railway from Vólos.
27km from Vólos.

Mousío Miléai (Milies Museum)

Exhibition of local costume and folkways.
On the main street above the square.
Tel: (242) 308 6204. Open: daily
10am–2pm. Free admission.

Tsangarádha

Tsangarádha's scattered squares are connected by steep cobbled steps and rushing streams. This is the prettiest of the eastern Pelion villages, looking out over the steep forests towards the silhouette of Skiathos on the eastern horizon. Its landmark is an enormous plane tree, 18m round and said to be 1,000 years old.
38km east of Vólos.

Vizítsa

At the end of a steeply winding road from the coast, Vizítsa is built around two huge flagstoned squares under the

shelter of enormous plane trees and is full of the sound of running water. Villagers gather at café tables in the afternoon and evening to play backgammon and drink *tsipouro*, a fiery grape spirit.
31km south of Vólos.

Vólos

Vólos, the gateway to the Pelion, is Greece's third port after Piraeus and Thessaloníki. A mainly industrial town at the head of the Pagasitic Gulf, it was rebuilt on a rigid grid pattern after being flattened by an earthquake in 1955.
355km north of Athens.

Mousío Arkheologikoú
(Vólos Archaeological Museum)

Hundreds of Hellenistic tombstones, carved with everyday scenes, are the centrepiece of a collection (due to return in spring 2004 after renovation) which also includes Stone Age

implements and Mycenaean pottery.
N Plastira 22. Tel: (242) 102 5285.
Open: Tue–Sun 8.30am–3pm.
Admission charge.

Mousío Theophiloú
(Theophilos Museum)

This mansion is decorated with vibrant primitive frescoes of robbers, priests, pashas and warriors, the work of the self-taught painter Theophilos, who spent much of his life roaming the Pelion.
Off Eleftherias, Nea Vólos. Tel: (242) 104 9109. Open: daily 8.30am–3pm.
Free admission.

Sidherodhrómo Píliou (Pelion Railway)

The narrow-gauge tracks you can see weaving along Vólos's waterfront and out of town towards Pelion are a relic of the Pelion railway, built in the last century. Two tiny locomotives and their miniature carriages can be seen rusting in sidings at the main railway station.

The port of Vólos at the head of the Pagasitic Gulf, looked down upon from the Pelion peninsula

Tour: Villages of Zagória

The stone-built villages of the Zagória region with their grey-slabbed roofs stand among the most exciting mountain scenery in Greece. Tourism is a relative newcomer, encouraged by newly built roads. The region is traversed by deep canyons, crossed in many places by graceful arched bridges built without the use of mortar. Wildlife abounds. Look out for griffon vultures circling the high peaks and for tortoises crossing the road.

Allow 6 hours.

Start 18km north of Ioánnina, leaving the main Ioánnina-Kónitsa road at Kariaí, and follow the signposted road towards Tsepélovon.

At each junction follow the signs to Tsepélovon.

Arkoudis Memorial

Twenty-six kilometres from the Kariaí junction, a roadside plaque commemorates the guerrilla leader Yioryios Arkoudis, 'killed by a Turkish bullet' here in 1906 when this part of Greece was still under the rule of the Turks.

A modern bridge crosses the confluence of two river beds 1km further on. A steeply arched old bridge stands next to it, between sheer cliff walls.

You are now entering the heart of the Zagória canyon country, a challenge for even the most seasoned trekker. The river bed, dry for most of the year, becomes a torrent in winter and early spring.

The road climbs for 8km towards Kepésovon, perched on the lip of the canyon.

Kipoi (Kipi)

Before reaching Kepésovon, you can turn right and detour for 4km to the village of Kipoi, to view the triple-arched bridge crossing the ravine 1km west of the village.

Just after the Kepésovon turning, pull off the road and look across the gorge to where a little-used mule path zigzags perilously down the cliff face. These cobbled paths, most of which have fallen into disrepair with the building of modern roads, were the highways of the region.
Drive for another 5km.

Rongovos Monastery

The monastery and church of Áyios Ioánnis are well worth the 10-minute walk from the road, even if a monkish caretaker is not in residence. The view into the canyon below is breathtaking.
3km beyond the monastery and 30km from the main Ioánnina-Kónitsa road, Tsepélovon is the biggest and most atmospheric of the Zagória villages.

Tsepélovon

Two gigantic plane trees shade a flagstoned square, Platia Stratigou Tsakalotou Thrasyvoulou, and its three old-fashioned cafés. At one end of the square stands a six-sided stone clock tower built in 1868 and behind it is the attractive colonnaded church of Áyios Nikolaos, built in 1871 and lavishly decorated within. Many of Tsepélovon's older houses are derelict, but are being restored.
From Tsepélovon the road passes through pine forests to Skamnéllion, then through alpine scenery for some 15km

below limestone peaks, sparsely covered with pine trees, before dropping to the red-roofed village of Vrisokhórion.

Vrisokhórion (Vrisohori)

Built on either side of a fertile, shel-tered valley, the village is a mountain oasis of garden terraces and walnut trees among oak woods. The substantial arcaded church of Áyios Xralampos with its carved stone doorway and mosaic floors is typical of Zagória village churches.
Between Amfipolis and the coastal highway, the road ends 3km from Vrisokhórion at the bottom of a steep canyon. A concrete road bridge connecting Vrisokhórion with Kónitsais is being built but the roads are poorly maintained and a 4-wheel drive is recommended.

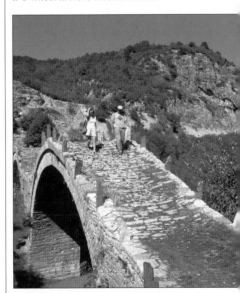

The three-arched bridge at Kipi is the finest of the Zagória pack-bridges

Goats and Goatherds

The tinkling of goatbells across a silent mountain valley is one of the unforgettably evocative sounds of Greece. Nobody whose car has been stopped and surrounded by a herd of goats being driven across the road will forget the smell, either.

The goat, like the forest fire, played its part in the deforestation of Greece, reducing most mountainsides to barren, rocky terrain that only a goat could love.

Like everything else in Greece, the goat is a political issue, with environmentalists condemning a 1980s government decision to allow grazing on national forest land devastated by fire – a move which may perhaps have encouraged firebugs to burn off still more trees for goat pasture.

The goat is still central to survival for many mountain villagers, and herders drive their flocks from lower slopes into the high peaks in summer to take advantage of pastures watered by melting snow.

Hill-walkers will meet goatherds in the most unpromising-looking locations, and their corrals of dry-stone walls, thorns, and corrugated iron (called *stanes*) are useful landmarks in the Greek high country.

Many of the goatherds who pasture their flocks in the Píndhos mountains of northern Epirus are Vlachs, members of a dwindling ethnic minority who speak a language closely related to Romanian, and whose ancestors are said to have been Roman legionaries who guarded the mountain passes in ancient times.

Others are descended from the Sarakatsan clans, who until the early years of this century lived a truly nomadic existence. You can see their colourful rugs and embossed silver jewellery in many of the region's folk museums.

Goat meat rarely turns up on tourist menus, and even in Greek homes it is a dish for special occasions such as Easter and Panayiria, the feast of the Assumption of the Virgin (15 August).

Greek goats find a meal wherever they can

Makedhonía and Thráki

Macedonia and Thrace

Greece's northernmost provinces border Bulgaria, Turkey and the former Yugoslav republic of Macedonia, and their remoter regions are still comparatively untouched by the modern world.

Macedonia, hemmed in to the west and south by the great mountain ranges of the north Píndhos and Olympus, has a strong identity of its own. Its people are often taller and fairer than their southern compatriots and are often blue- or grey-eyed. Their huge province includes fertile valleys watered by Greece's biggest rivers, huge lakes, the highest mountain in Greece, the country's second city and – on the triple peninsulas of Khalkidhikí – a self-governing theocracy and some of the country's best and as yet totally unspoilt beaches.

Thrace, lying further east, clearly shows its Turkish heritage in the music, dress, arts and crafts of its large Muslim minority. Its flat coastal plain shimmers in the summer sun, growing bumper crops of grain, cotton and tobacco, minarets shoot skyward from many of its sleepy villages, and storks and pelicans haunt the reedbeds and lagoons along its coast. Of all the regions of Greece, Thrace is the least touched by tourism, depending for its livelihood instead on agriculture. In these flat farmlands the traditional two-wheeled donkey cart is still one of the most popular means of transport.

A combination of little-visited towns and villages and some splendid rugged mountain country in the north of the region makes Thrace one of Greece's best-kept secrets.

Since 1987 archeological excavations have thrown more light on the early life and customs of the people of this region.

What's in a Name?

With the break-up of Yugoslavia, Greece claimed sole rights to the name Macedonia and did everything it could to block recognition of the province's northern neighbour, the former Yugoslavian republic of Macedonia, as the Republic of Macedonia. Though the campaign seems to have been lost, it is still a touchy subject and, like other topics which touch on the fierce Greek national pride, best avoided.

Macedonia and Thrace

The commercial port of Kavala, surmounted by its Byzantine castle

EASTERN MACEDONIA AND THRACE

Amfipoli (Amfipolis)

The fortifications of this impressive 5th-century BC city are being excavated and restored, as are the mosaic floors of its Christian basilica.

Between Amfipolis and the coastal highway, overlooking the Strimón (Strimonas) River, stands a monumental stone lion, pieced together in 1937 from fragments recovered from the river bed. It dates from the late 4th century BC.

Signposted north of the Kavala-Thessaloníki highway, 60km southwest of Kaválla (Kavala). Free access.

Évros Delta

The Évros drains into a wide delta of salt lagoons and sluggish channels where seabirds, including pelicans, abound.

13–15km east of Alexandroúpolis. Turn off the main road at Loutra Traianopolis on to a network of dirt roads.

Filippi (Philippi)

The most impressive survivals of this town, founded in the 4th century BC, are the broad, paved expanse of the Roman agorá and the arches and columns of the Christian basilica, begun in the 6th century but never completed because it was too big to support its dome. The town is particularly famous because it was here that Octavian (the future Roman Emperor Augustus) and Mark Anthony defeated Brutus and Cassius, the murderers of Julius Caesar, in 42 BC, and because it was at Philippi that the Apostle Paul established the first Christian community in Europe.

On the opposite side of the road is a theatre, carved out of the hillside in the 4th century BC and now used for performances in summer, and the remains of another basilica, built in about AD 500.

18km northwest of Kaválla.

Kaválla (Kavala)

Turkish-style houses with shutters, tiled roofs and overhanging second storeys clutter the winding cobbled streets, which ascend from Kavala's busy commercial harbour to its Byzantine castle. The Apostle Paul landed here on his first missionary journey to Europe, and it was here that Mehmet Ali (1769–1849) was born, who became Pasha of Egypt and whose last descendant as ruler of Egypt was King Farouk (abdicated 1952).

170km east of Thessaloníki.

Anapsihtirio Imaret (Turkish Almshouse)

A forest of domes and chimney-pots marks this derelict building above the harbour. Built to house the poor of the city by Mehmet Ali, its cool courtyard with its whitewashed arcades is now a pleasant café-bar adorned with relics of old Kavala.

Opposite junction of Theod Poulidou and Mohamet-Ali.

Arkheologiko Mousío (Kavala Archaeological Museum)

Finds include delicate polychrome glass vases, reliefs and mosaics from Amfipolis, gilded jewellery and a restored 250 BC Macedonian tomb chamber.

Erithrou Stavrou, in a small park at the western end of the harbour esplanade.

*Tel: (251) 022 2335 Open: Tue–Sun
8.30am–3pm. Admission charge.*

Kástro (Castle)

The Byzantine citadel was taken over
and expanded by the Turks. An
impressive aqueduct, which supplied the
citadel and the town below with water,
crosses the main Kavala-Alexan-
dhroupolis road below the castle.
*Tel: (251) 083 8602. Open: Tue–Sun
8.30am–5pm. Free admission.*

Komotiní

A quaint mixture of modern and
traditional, Komotiní is a market town
with a strong ethnic Muslim element.
Look out for women in chador-like
black dresses and headscarves and older
men in soft skullcaps in the open-air
market held every Tuesday. The bazaar
area in the street either side of
pedestrianised Venizelou is fascinating.
113km east of Kaválla.

Mousío Morphotikou Omilou Komotinis
(Museum of Folk Life and History)

Collection of domestic items and folk
costumes, with fine examples of local
wedding embroidery.
*Ayíou Yioryiou 13. Open: Mon–Sat
10am–1pm.*

Yeni Came (Yeni Mosque)

The mosque and its graceful minaret
stand next to a 19th-century clock tower
bearing an inscription from the Koran.
Behind the mosque stand the
headstones and tombs of a Turkish
graveyard.
Venizelou 83/Platia Ifaistou.

Xánthi

Xánthi's wealth traditionally came from
tobacco trading, and its prosperity is
reflected by the large mansions in its old
quarter, many now restored.
56km east of Kaválla.

Laografiko Mousío (Folk Art Museum)

The museum is housed in a recently
restored, splendidly decorated tobacco
baron's house with painted ceilings.
Displays include weapons, copper and
brassware, and gorgeous rugs from
Sarakatsan.
*Antika 7. Tel: (254) 102 5421.
Open: Mon, Wed, Thu & weekends,
11am–1pm & 6.30–8.30pm.
Admission charge.*

Palaio Xánthi (Old Xanthi)

The old quarter, with its largely car-free
cobbled streets and yellow and white
stuccoed houses, stands above the
modern town centre.
North of Vasilissis Sofias.

A restored tobacco trader's mansion in Xanthi's
old quarter

KHALKIDHIKÍ

Shaped like a three-fingered hand, Khalkidhikí points south into the Aegean. The easternmost peninsula, closed to tourists, is Áyion Óros (Holy Mountain/Mount Athos), a semi-independent territory ruled by the abbots of its score of monasteries (*see* the Mount Athos tour, *pp130–31*) and dominated by the sharp-edged peak of Athos, 2,033m high, on its southern tip.

Kassándhra, the furthest west of the three peninsulas and the closest to Thessaloníki's international airport is, not surprisingly, the biggest tourism puller, with a necklace of resorts catering to holidaymakers from all over Europe.

It is worth spending one night on the west coast for the glowing sunsets, with the peaks of Olympus, Óssa and Pílion (Pelion) silhouetted on the opposite shore of the Thermaïkós Kólpos (Thermaic Gulf), some 50–60km away.

Sithonía (Sidhonia), the middle peninsula, is less developed and more rugged than its western neighbour. Thick pine forest alternates with bare boulders and the scars of forest fires. Sidhonia's east coast has some of the best and least crowded beaches in Greece. Its southern tip is barren and blasted by winter gales and summer heat.

Néa Fókaia

The small square keep of Áyios Pavlos (St Paul) guards a pleasant, east-facing sandy beach with three summer *tavérnas*.
8km south of Néa Potidhia on Kassándhra's east coast.
The tower is not open.

Néa Potídhaia (Nea Potidhia)

The gateway to Kassándhra, where a narrow canal has been cut through the isthmus to allow yachts to pass through.
80km southeast of Thessaloníki.

Olinthos

An extensive complex of walls and pits on a flat-topped hill marks the site of ancient Olinthos, destroyed by Philip II of Macedon, father of Alexander, in 348 BC. He did a thorough job.

A 14th-century towered fortress guards the harbour at Ouranópolis

North of the main road, 4km west of Néa Moudhaniá and 1km from the village of Nea Olinthos. Tel: (237) 109 1280. Open: daily, except Mon, 8.30am–3pm. Admission charge.

Ouranópolis

The departure-point for cruises around the Áyion Óros and for pilgrims heading for the monasteries is a bustling little port with a pretty location on the Singitikós Kólpos/Kólpos Ayíou Orous (Gulf of the Holy Mountain). You can hire a boat to explore the small islands offshore. Ferries run frequently to Amoliani, the island opposite the harbour. A 14th-century fortress tower guards the harbour.
10km south of the isthmus linking the Áyion Óros to the mainland.

Palioúrion (Paliouri)

A chain of beach resorts runs up the east coast of Kassándhra from Paliouri, close to the peninsula's southern tip. There are many good sandy beaches with a backdrop of pine-clad hills, and the scenery is outstanding.
58km south of Néa Moudhania.

Petralona

Halfway between Thessaloníki and Kassándhra are the beautiful stalagmite and stalactite caves of Petralona, with colours ranging from pure white to deep red. The caves were inhabited in palaeolithic times, and contain the earliest known traces of man-made fire, dated to 700,000 years ago.
North of Eleohoria, on the N Kalikratitia – N Moudhaniá road. Open: Tue–Sun 8.30am–3pm. Admission charge.

Porto Carras

A self-contained complex of three enormous, obtrusive and charmless hotels overlooking a yacht marina, riding centre and golf course.
Midway along the west coast of Sidhonia. Tel: (237) 507 1381; www.portocarras.com

Sárti

A small resort popular with holidaymakers from Thessaloníki, Sárti stands by a sandy beach at the mouth of a green valley. Lots of *tavérnas* and discos indicate an active nightlife in summer.
On the east coast of Sidhonia, about 30km from its southern tip.

Sikéas (Sikias)

A triangle of farmland forms a fertile oasis of fields and orchards hemmed in by low, jagged hills behind a long curve of sandy, little-visited beach.
On the east coast of Sidhonia, about 20km from the southern tip.

Torone (Toroni)

Toroni could not be more different from its big neighbour. This tiny resort has 2km of sandy beach on a wide west-facing bay, with a backdrop of barren, rocky hills.
5km south of Porto Carras.

Vourvourou

Vourvourou is set on a shallow, almost landlocked lagoon overlooking a calm bay with a scattering of tiny islands. There are sandy beaches either side of the small village.
On the east coast of Sidhonia, close to its northern end.

THESSALONÍKI

Greece's second city was largely destroyed by fire in 1917 and struck by an earthquake in 1978, so it comes as some surprise that so many ancient and medieval buildings survive. Built on a long crescent bay at the head of the Thermaïkós Kólpos (Thermaic Gulf), it is a lively city, with smart shops, lots of good restaurants and fashionable cafés, and an energetic nightlife.

Akrópolis (Acropolis)

Sections of the city's 4th-century ramparts, extended and reinforced by the Byzantines in the 14th century and the Turks in the 15th, partially enclose the old quarter. The most imposing remnants of the medieval fortifications are the Dingirle Koule (Chain Tower), a twin of the Lefkos Pirgos (White Tower) on the seafront, and the recently restored section of walls between the

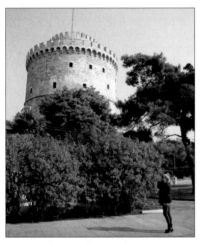

The White Tower on the waterfront is Thessaloníki's most prominent landmark

Pirgos Palaiologos and the Pirgos Andronikos towers, dating from the 14th century.
Enter the old quarter at the Dingirle Koule, at the northeast end of Zografou.

Apsis Galeriou (Arch of Galerius)

The 4th-century arch was built at the crossroads of Roman Thessaloníki to honour the Emperor Galerius. It stands beside one of the city's busiest streets and is being restored.
Corner of Egnatia and Gounari.

Arkheologikó Mousíou (Archaeological Museum)

The stupendous finds from the royal Macedonian tombs at Vergína (*see p129*) are the central attraction of this fine museum. The workmanship and materials testify to the wealth and sophistication of ancient Macedon. Among the most striking are the tiny ivory heads of Philip II and Alexander, beautifully wrought gold jewellery, the embossed gold funerary chests and delicate ornamental wreaths, the bronze, silver and gold shields and cauldrons, and the skeleton of Philip II.
Junction of d'Esperey and Stratou. Tel: (231) 083 0538. Open: Mon 11am–5pm, Tue–Fri 8am–5pm, weekends & holidays 8.30am–3pm. Admission charge.

Áyios Dhimítrios

The church, originally built in the 5th century but extensively rebuilt since then, is the largest in Greece. It contains the relics of St Dhimitrios, the city's patron saint, who was executed by the Emperor Galerius at that spot in AD 306.

Upper side of Platia Dikastirion. Tel: (231) 027 0008. Open: Tue–Sun 8.30am–3pm. Free admission.

Áyia Sofia

Like Áyios Dhimitrios, this 8th-century church became a mosque with the Turkish conquest. Now a church again, its dim candlelit interior is decorated with painted domes, restored *trompe-l'œil* mosaics and richly ornamented screens.

Midway along Egnatia, between Egnatia and Tsimiski. Open: daily 8.30am–12.30pm, 5–7.30pm. Free admission.

Áyios Yeóryios/Áyios Yiorgios (Rotonda)

The squat, massive building was intended to be the tomb of the Roman Emperor Galerius, was converted into a church in the following century, and became a mosque under the Turks.

Filippou, 50m north of the Apsis Galeriou (Arch of Galerius). Open: Tue–Fri 8.30am–7pm, Sat & Sun 8.30am–3pm.

Bedestan (Old Market)

The Ottoman-period market area off Venizelou is a chaos of stalls and shops selling everything under the sun. Noisy and colourful, it is a photographer's delight. Go early in the morning to catch it in full swing.

Laografiko-Ethnologiko Mousíon Makedhonias (Folklife-Ethnological Museum of Macedonia)

A collection of costumes, artefacts and photographs illustrating the vanished folk art and life of northern Greece,

The doorway of Thessaloníki's 8th-century church of Áyia Sofia

housed in a 19th-century mansion near the waterfront. There is an interesting display on the traditional *karaghiosis* (shadow-puppet theatre).

Vass. Olgas 68. Tel: (231) 083 0591. Open: Fri–Wed 9.30am–2pm. Admission charge.

Levkos Pirgos (White Tower)

The 35-m circular tower on the waterfront was a bastion of the Byzantine city walls, rebuilt by the Turks in about 1430, and used mainly as a prison. It houses an excellent Byzantine museum with some very striking icons, tombs, mosaics and frescoes. The top storey houses a pleasant, cool café whose rooftop terrace offers a fine view of the town and the harbour.

East end of Leoforos Nikis. Tel: (231) 026 7832. Open: Tue–Sun 8.30am–3pm. Free admission.

flotillas of one-man craft (sometimes towed behind a larger vessel) usually set out at sundown, to come puttering back with their catch at first light.

Some 5,000 years of intensive fishing have taken their toll of the Aegean's stocks, and Greek boatmen have long used everything from fine-mesh nets to fish-traps and tridents.

In more recent times, dynamite became a potent and popular way of maximising results, and it is not uncommon to meet fishermen who have lost a hand through a mishap with explosives.

With such a comprehensive approach, it is hardly surprising that the catch is increasingly small and mostly made up of tiddlers. Nets full of whitebait, sprats and mackerel are common, but the prized *barbounia* (red mullet) commands a far higher price.

No Greek harbour is complete without its complement of tiny, brightly painted fishing boats and lengths of crimson-dyed net spread out to dry.

Look closely at the prow of many of these little vessels and you will see, cut into the wood, a diamond-shape – a stylised modern version of the painted eye with which the ancient Greeks decorated their galleys.

Most fishing is done at night, and

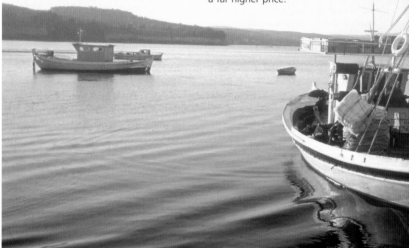

Bigger fish like tunny and swordfish are often caught off the southern Peloponnese, in the deep waters of the Steno Kíthiro (Kithira Channel).

Boats fitted with powerful acetylene lamps are used to attract squid into a circle of nets, while octopus are caught with a trident or a formidable triple hook on a hand-line.

Greece's lakes, too, have their fishing fleets. On Límni Ioánninon (Lake Pamvotis), Límni Kastorías (Lake Kastoria) and the Límni Préspes (Prespa lakes), as well as on the reservoirs formed by Greece's many hydro-electric dams, local fishers set out after carp and other freshwater fish in black-tarred punts.

And on Greece's beaches, fishers of another kind trawl for a different catch: young Greek men who spend their summers in romantic pursuit of female tourists are called *kamaki* – 'harpooners'.

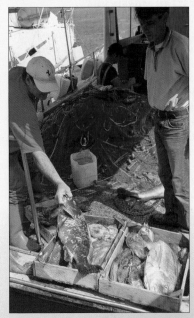

Above: the catch of the day is separated and arranged appetisingly by some fishermen
Below: fishing boat at anchor

WESTERN MACEDONIA
Dhíon
Highlights of the most impressive site in Macedonia are the marble and mosaic floors of the baths, the Sanctuary of Isis with copies of the original statues, and a length of the cobbled road to Olympus.
115km south of Thessaloníki. The site is 2km east of Dhíon village.
Tel: (235) 105 3206.
Open: daily 8am–5pm. Admission charge.

Mousío (Museum)
The museum has a rich and well-displayed collection of statues, coins, jewellery and everyday objects and an excellent explanatory video programme.
Signposted in the centre of Dhíon village.
Tel: (235) 105 3206. Open: daily 8am–5pm. Admission charge covers both site and museum.

Kastoría
Surrounded on three sides by its lake, Kastoría is one of the prettiest towns in Greece. It grew wealthy on the fur trade, and though the beavers which gave it its name (*castor* is Latin for beaver) have disappeared, small factories still make up the distinctive patchwork fur garments for which the town is known. Grand 19th-century fur-merchants' mansions stand on the slope overlooking the lake, southeast of the modern town centre.
210km west of Thessaloníki.

Koumbelidhíki Panagía
The most important of Kastoría's antique churches has striking exterior frescoes of Salome and John the Baptist. Decorative brickwork, interspersing geometric rows of brick with masonry, is a feature of all Kastoría's Byzantine churches.
Off Caravagelli. Closed for renovation but opened on request.
Tel: (246) 702 6781/6777.

Laografikó Mousío Kastoriás (Kastoría Folk Museum)
On the ground floor of this fur-trader's mansion are barrel-filled cellars, a green courtyard with the kitchen and a copper still. The upper floors have elaborately decorated woodwork, polished floors and painted ceilings.
Kapetan 10. Open: daily 8.30am–6pm. Admission charge.

Mousío Byzantikón (Byzantine Museum)
The museum's collection of glowing crimson and gold icons is one of the best in Greece. Unfortunately, all texts and explanations are in Greek.
Off V Iperiou, next to the Xenia hotel.
Open: Tue–Sun 8.30am–3pm. Admission charge.

Límni Préspes (Prespa Lakes)
Megali Préspa (Great Prespa) and Mikrí Préspa (Little Prespa) are a refuge for pelicans, storks, egrets, spoonbills and cormorants. Around them stand a handful of villages which seem to have been barely touched by the 20th century.
190km northwest of Thessaloníki.

Ólimbos Óros (Mount Olympus)
The tallest mountain in Greece (2,817m) and the legendary home of the gods dominates Macedonia and the north from most angles. The peak is usually covered in cloud by midday, adding to its air of mystery. (*Also see p140*).

Pélla

The ancient capital of Macedonia, Pélla was also the childhood home of Alexander the Great. Mosaics of warriors in battle, stag hunts, and the abduction of Helen by Paris (*see p57*) have been perfectly preserved under layers of silt. Also worth seeing are the columns of the Colonnade of the Court. Excavations are continuing, and a viewing-tower gives you a bird's-eye view of this extensive Macedonian site.

The museum, on the opposite side of the road from the site, has an excellent collection of marbles and some lovely fluid pebble-mosaics and terracotta statuettes.

On the main road between Thessaloníki and Yiannitsá (Yianitsa), 39km west of Thessaloníki. Tel: (238) 203 1160. Open: daily 8.30am–3pm. Admission charge covers site and museum.

Vergína

The **tombs** identified as those of Philip II of Macedon and other members of his family make this the most significant site unearthed this century. Above ground, the remains of the **royal palace** include a magnificent mosaic floor with stylised floral and geometric patterns. Below it, the magnificent marble-lined royal tombs with their great stone sarcophagi cannot fail to impress, though the treasures of the tombs – and Philip II's remains – are in the Thessaloníki Archaeological Museum. A smaller tomb, beneath an unsightly metal roof, is between the palace and the village.

Anaktora (Palace): near Palatitsia, signposted 2km from modern Vergína, Tombs: signposted on the outskirts of Vergína. Tel: (233) 109 2347. Open: Tue–Sun 8.30am–3pm. Admission charge.

Mount Olympus, the highest mountain in Greece, chosen by the gods for their home

Tour: Áyion Óros (Mount Athos)

Mount Athos, the Holy Mountain, has been ruled by its monks since the 10th century. Special permission from the Ministry of Northern Greece is required to visit the 45-km long peninsula, and women – and even female animals – are banned. Around 1,500 monks now live in the 20 monasteries. Each monastery is ruled by its abbot and each is built in a distinctively different architectural style. Some perch on the slopes of the mountain, others stand beside natural harbours.

The monasteries of the west coast can be clearly observed from the cruise ships which sail daily from the small port of Ouranópolis, just north of the frontier between the Holy Mountain and the outside world.

Snacks, drinks and camera film are sold on board. Boats must stay at least 500m offshore, so a zoom lens and binoculars are useful.

Tickets are sold in advance by agencies on the Ouranópolis harbourfront, and the trip takes 4 to 6 hours.

A multi-lingual commentary (English/ German/Greek) is provided.

Leaving Ouranópolis the boat cruises southeast along the barren coast of the peninsula.

Dhokhiaríou (Dohiariou)

Easily spotted by its crenellated defence tower, this monastery on the seashore was built in the 10th century. One of the less inhabited monasteries, it now has around a dozen monks.

Xenofóndos (Xenophontos)

Named after its 10th-century founder, St Xenofon, the fortress-like building overlooks a long pebbly strand. Damaged by pirates and fires, it has frequently been rebuilt and is a patchwork of styles.

Áyíou Pandeleímonos (Áyios Panteleimonas)

Most striking and colourful of all, with scarlet walls and green onion-domes, each surmounted by a gold orb and cross, the present monastery was built by Russian monks in the late 18th century.

Xiropotámou (Xeropotamos)

High on a ridge above the coast, Xiropotámou overlooks the tiny harbour at Dháfni. One of the most modern monasteries, it has been rebuilt a number of times over the last three centuries after a series of disastrous fires.

Dháfni (Dafni)

Below Xiropotámou, Dháfni is the peninsula's official harbour and entry-point for pilgrims. The mountain's only road runs from the port to Kariaí (Karies), the administrative capital of Mount Athos.

Símonos Pétras (Simonopetra)

Perched dizzyingly on its crag, Simonos Pétras is unmistakable, a seven-storey building which seems to grow straight out of the cliff.

Osíou Grigoríou (Gregoriou)

Another clifftop eyrie, Grigoríou is dedicated to St Nicholas and is the smallest of the Athos monasteries. With binoculars you can clearly see its cheerfully colourful red-tiled roof and blue balconies overlooking the sea.

Dhionisíou (Dionysiou)

The fortress-like 14th-century building is easily recognised by its tiers of white and pink balconies, 80m above the sea. The interior contains some fine frescoes.

Ayou Pávlou (Áyios Pavlos)

High above the sea, Ayíou Pávlou is a dour stone building cradled by outcrops of the peak of Mount Athos.

Áyion Óros (Mount Athos)

While the whole peninsula is known by this name, the peak itself is at its southern tip. Its steep slopes drop sheer into the sea and the summit towers to a height of 2,033m.

From the southern tip, the boat returns to Ouranópolis.

Amolianí

Most excursion boats stop at this small island, about 20 minutes from Ouranópolis, where a pretty harbour offers a choice of *tavérnas*. There is a beach about 10 minutes' walk from the harbourside.

Permission to visit the holy mountain is usually granted only to Orthodox pilgrims or scholars with a special interest in Greece. For further information contact the Ministry of Northern Greece, Platia Dhikitiriou, Thessaloníki. *Tel: (231) 027 0092.*

'When Alexander saw the breadth of his domain he wept for there were no more worlds to conquer.' Though the authorship of this quote has not yet been definitively determined, history has proven that conquest and warfare ruled the restless Alexander throughout his short life.

Separated from the warring city-states of the southern mainland by mountain ranges, Macedon was thought of by civilised Hellenes as a near-barbarous land.

But the disastrous Peloponnesian War (431–404 BC) between Athens and Sparta drew in all the cities of the south and spelt the beginning of the end of their era.

As their political, military and economic power waned, Macedon became a power to be reckoned with.

Philip II, Alexander's father, used his genius to develop the Macedonian war machine, which reached the acme of its brilliance under Alexander. At the battle of Khairónia in 338 BC, (see p86), Philip's Macedonians shattered the combined forces of the southern cities, using radically new tactics. Against the swords and shield-wall of the south, Philip threw a phalanx of pike-wielding infantry backed up by heavy cavalry.

Commanding the cavalry wing was his 18-year-old son, Alexander. Two years later, following Philip's assassination, he became king and began the meteoric career which made him a legend.

Alexander had been groomed in the warrior skills of Macedon and in the finer arts of civilised Greece, the philosopher Aristotle having been his tutor, but he is remembered above all as a brilliant general. A year after his father's death, Alexander crushed a revolt by the Thebans and sacked their city, consolidating Macedon's control of the Greek mainland.

In 334 BC he invaded Asia Minor, defeating a Persian army on the River Granikos, and six years later all Persia was his. Pushing east, he took Sogdiana (Uzbekistan), Bactria (Afghanistan), and reached India, but his exhausted soldiers refused to go further.

Returning to Persia in 324 BC, he planned to forge Persia and Greece into one empire, but met strong opposition. Before he could overcome it, he died of fever. He was 33 years old.

His empire quickly collapsed as his generals set up kingdoms for themselves in the east, though Macedon remained the major power in Greece until Rome defeated its last independent king, Perseus, at Pydna in 167 BC.

Facing page: an image of the youthful Alexander
Below: Alexander the Great fights Hindus and Persians at Ephesus (15th-century manuscript)

Getting Away From It All

The Flying Dolphins cruise the Argo-Saronic seas

'It was a land of scintillating diversity, a cornucopia of riches. It was almost part of the mainland, but not quite. It was an island, but an island apart from the rest. And it was only two hours from Athens.'

SARA WHEELER
An Island Apart, 1993

ARGO-SARONIC ISLANDS

Frequent fast hydrofoils bring the beaches and pretty villages of these attractive islands close to Athens. Hellas Flying Dolphins Hydrofoils provide services to and from the islands and their offices are situated at Akti Kondili, Piraews (*tel: (210) 419 9100; www.dolphins.gr*). Journey times from Piraeus range from half an hour to two hours. It is also possible to take a one-day cruise of the Saronic Islands. Boats leave the Athenian port of Paleo Faliro early morning and cruise around Aegina, Poros and Hydra, returning to Athens early evening (*see p140*).

Aíyina (Aegina)

The largest of the Argo-Saronic islands and the closest to Athens, Aegina is a favourite weekend resort of Athenians wanting peace and quiet. Visit Aegina to swim, eat at seafood *tavérnas* and visit the temple.

Naós Aphaía (Temple of Aphaia)

The Doric temple to Aphaia, protectress of women, retains most of its 32 columns.
40 minutes from Athens, on the hilltop

close to the northeast tip of the island. Tel: (229) 703 2398. Open: Mon–Fri 8am–5pm, weekends 8.30am–3pm. Admission charge.

Angístrion

A tiny island with one little fishing-harbour-cum-resort, Angístrion seems much more remote than it is. Only a few hundred metres from Aegina, its beaches are usually much less crowded. Come here to do nothing except swim, sunbathe and relax.
30 minutes from Aíyina by boat.

Ídhra (Hydra)

Rows of whitewashed mansions rise above a port crowded with fancy yachts and cruisers as well as the inevitable fishing boats. There are no roads outside the village, but there are coves and pebbly beaches for swimming within walking distance of the village.
1 hour & 40 minutes from Athens.

Póros

A stone's throw from the mainland, the village is a multicoloured clutter of houses and the harbour bustles with hydrofoils and ferries. There are good

beaches on the mainland opposite, and small boats shuttle to and fro every few minutes.
1 hour from Athens.

Spétsai

Spétsai sits at the mouth of the Argolikós Kólpos (Argolic Gulf) a short hop from the mainland. The village is an attractive mix of 18th-century shipowners' mansions and neo-classical 19th-century buildings, surrounding two harbours, the older fishing port and the newer harbour, where ferries and hydrofoils dock. Much of the island is covered by pine woods and there are pleasant walks and good beaches.
2–2½ hours from Athens.

Évvoia (Evia)

Greece's second-largest island is only a couple of hours away from Athens via frequent ferry services from Rafína and Marmári and Káristos, a small resort near the south tip, which has an enormous pebble beach, a ruined Turkish castle and lots of seaside *tavérnas.* You can also get to Evia by car,

as a swing bridge connects it to the mainland at Khalkís (Khalkidha) (*see map on p44*).

Levkás

This delightful Ionian island is connected to the mainland by a long causeway.

There are beautiful white beaches on the west coast and an archipelago of uninhabited islands dotted around the sheltered waters of the east coast (*see map on pp98–9*).

Skíathos

The pine-covered island of Skíathos has some of Greece's finest sandy beaches, and its beautiful island capital with its Italianate clock towers and red-tiled houses is a package-holiday favourite.
Daily hydrofoil services from Vólos in summer.

Thásos

Thásos is a huge, pine-covered island only an hour by the frequent ferry service from Kaválla. It has excellent sandy beaches.

Houses abutting the harbour at Hydra

BIRDWATCHING

The rivers and wetlands of the Greek mainland offer some of the finest birdwatching in Europe.

Akhelóös

The vast expanse of the Akhelóös delta is one of the finest birdwatching areas in Greece. The river reaches the sea through a maze of channels, among reedbeds, lagoons, cotton and maize fields and stands of eucalyptus. The shoreline is a marshy patchwork of lagoons, salt-pans and shallow, muddy bays. Kingfishers, larks and wagtails infest the river channels, and nearer the shoreline you can expect to see herons, egrets, many gull species, cormorants and terns.

About 30km from Mesolóngion (see p94).

Angelokhorión

The salt-pans at Angelokhorion, near Thessaloníki, attract Mediterranean gulls, slender-billed gulls and Audouin's gull in spring and autumn, as well as many kinds of wader and tern. You may also spot Cory's shearwater flying close inshore.

Near Ayía Triás, southeast of Thessaloníki.

Évros

The mud-flats and salt-marshes of the Évros delta attract waders of all kinds, herons, storks, pelicans, cormorants, plovers and larks.

About 30km east of Alexandhroupoli (see p120).

Límni Mikrí Préspa (Lake Mikri Prespa National Park)

Pelicans, pygmy cormorants, egrets, ibises and storks haunt the reedbeds of the remote lake. Huge flocks of jays can often be seen in the beech woods surrounding the lake.

35km north of Kastoría (see p129).

Dhion Archaeological Park is a great place for wildlife watching

Stork's nest on a telephone pole

Límni Vistonis (Lake Vistonis)

Salt-pans and a lagoon lie south of the causeway which cuts Lake Vistonis in two, carrying the main road.

Another causeway leads to the island church of Áyios Nikolaos, which is an ideal vantage-point for spotting ibises, egrets, pygmy cormorants, pelicans and herons.

Midway between Xánthi and Komotiní (see p121).

Mesolóngion (Missolonghi)

The lagoon at Mesolóngion with its fish hatcheries and salt-pans attracts curlews and many other waders, avocets, black-winged stilts, terns and gulls, and Kentish plovers *(see pp94–5).*

Néstos River

Look out for herons, terns, gulls, waders and (very rarely) flamingoes among the lagoons just north of Keramotí, close to the mouth of the Néstos River.

East of Kaválla. Follow signs to Gravouna, then Keramoti.

Wildlife

The wild mountains of Greece are home to some of Europe's last wolves and bears, though you are most unlikely to see them. Wolves are claimed to be on the increase in the northern mountains and are ruthlessly hunted, getting the blame for attacks on flocks which are more likely to be the work of dogs. Bears are rare and very shy.

The same hill country which shelters these vanishing predators is also the home of the spectacular Griffon and the Lammergeier vultures, two of Europe's largest raptors, and of harriers, buzzards and golden eagles.

A variety of snakes, including vipers, smooth snakes and grass snakes, are common and killed impartially whether venomous or not. Rocky hillsides and stone walls are the haunt of many species of lizard, including several species of wall lizard and the larger, more vivid green lizard and the snake-eyed lizard. Geckos are found clinging to walls after dark and often gather around electric lights which attract the insects they feed on. Terrapins congregate in ponds and rivers, where they like to bask in sunny locations on banks and logs.

Land tortoises are found everywhere but are commonest in the Píndhos Óros (Píndhos mountains) and are all too frequently seen squashed on the road.

Flowers and Butterflies

Greece's rocky hillsides may look barren, but because they are little-cultivated they are a paradise for wild flowers.

Much of the country is deemed suitable only for goat pasture, and wild flowers are left to flourish without interference.

In addition, Greek farming is still piecemeal, allowing wild plants to thrive in fields, orchards and olive groves alongside cultivated plants.

The best time to see Greece in bloom is in spring (as early as March in the southern Peloponnese or as late as June in the north) when hillsides and plains are ablaze with red, yellow and purple. Wild orchids are abundant, as are cistus, anemones, poppies, irises, gladioli, vetches, crocuses and many others. Purple and blue morning glories cover ruined walls, and every watercourse is marked by the pink flowers of oleander. Even after the lower regions have been scorched dry by the summer sun, the high slopes of Taïyetos and Píndhos where melting snow prolongs the spring may be a happy hunting ground.

Greece's climate and soil suit many species of orchid. As early as February you can hope to spot the giant orchids (*Barlia sp.*) and some varieties of bee orchid in the southern Peloponnese, and mountain-loving helleborine orchids may be found on north-facing slopes as late as July.

Unfortunately, European Union subsidies are encouraging many Greek farmers to experiment with more intensive cultivation. As a result, crops in parts of the mainland are becoming less varied, reducing the opportunities for wild flowers to flourish.

The range of food plants available and the limited use of insecticides make Greece a butterfly heaven, and the vivid colours of butterfly wings are all the more readily spotted against the greys and browns of dry summer landscapes.

Among the most exotic butterfly

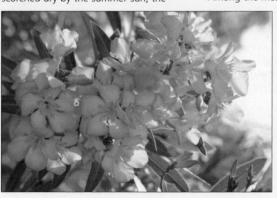

species are the huge, zebra-striped scarce swallowtail (*Iphiclides podalirius*), the southern swallowtail (*Papilio alexanor*), and the plain tiger (*Danaus chrysippus*). On hillsides, look out for the many different species of fast-flying fritillaries, and in fields and road verges watch for the flashing wings of more than a dozen species of blues.

The day-flying hummingbird hawk moth is a common denizen of flower gardens and fields, unmistakable because of its long, curling tongue and its ability to fly backwards with fast-beating wings. Its night-flying relatives, the huge poplar hawk moth, lime hawk moth and oleander hawk moth, are often drawn to unshaded lights after dark.

The countryside, ablaze with colour in summer with butterflies, bees, oleanders, cactus flowers and the common poppy and daisy

CLIMBING ÓLIMBOS ÓROS (MOUNT OLYMPUS)

Greece's mightiest mountain has nine peaks of more than 2,600m. The highest, Mitikas, reaches 2,917m.

Allow three days and two nights for the climb. Enter Ólimbos National Park from the village of Litokhoron, near the foot of the mountain, and drive, walk, hitch-hike or take a taxi to Prionia at 1,100m. From here a well-trodden trail zigzags steeply through pine woods to the Greek Alpine Club's Refuge A, a 3-hour hike. The refuge, at 2,100m, sleeps 90 people in bunk-bedded dormitories. Simple but filling meals are available.

Start for the summit immediately after breakfast, following a trail marked by metal arrows to Olympus's third-highest summit, Skala.

Do not attempt the final 200m separating Skala from Mitikas without an excellent head for heights and some climbing experience. On one side of the ridge between the two peaks there is a vertical, 500m drop. On the other, the path is no more than a series of holds.

Skolio, the mountain's second-highest peak, is an easy 750m walk from Skala. Allow 7 hours for the round trip from Refuge A to the summit and back.

Nights on Olympus are chilly and the days cool. Make sure you book accommodation in advance.The refuge provides blankets, but you should take a sweater and windproof jacket. Other essentials include a water-bottle, good boots and dried fruit or chocolate.
Ellinikos Oreivatikos Syllogos Litokhoron (Greek Alpine Club of Litokhoron), Kentriki Platia, 60200 Litokhoron. Tel: (235) 208 1944. Open: May–Oct

Cruises are essential for sightseeing

8am–noon & 4-6pm.
Spilios Agapitos (Refuge A): Tel: (235) 208 1800. Open: May–Oct 6am–10pm.

CRUISES

Among the most popular cruises are those taking in the delightful villages of the Cyclades islands. Cruises can be as short as one day or as long as a week, and can be arranged through any Athens travel agency or through major hotels.
Contact: **Dolphin Hellas Cruises** (Syngrou 16; *tel: (210) 922 7772; www.dolphin-hellas.gr*); or
Epirotiki Lines (Akti Miaouli 87, 185 38 Piraeus; *tel: (210) 429 1501; www.epirotiki.gr*).

Yachting

There are dozens of yacht charter companies in Greece, most of them based in and around Athens. Yachts can be chartered with or without a licensed crew. Suitable sailing weather is from April to October, though in August the strong Meltemi wind can keep boats in harbour for up to three days at a time.
A list of yacht charter companies is available from the Greek National Tourist Office (see p189).

The Olympus trail zigzags steeply through pine woods and treeless peaks

Shopping

There are bargains to be found, especially in Athens. If you are shopping for distinctive regional products – such as rugs and blankets from Arákhova or silverware from Ioánnina – you may find them cheaper in Athens than in the villages in which they are made. Shops traditionally open between 8am and 1pm, close until around 5pm then reopen until about 8pm, though in Athens many souvenir shops stay open all day and late into the night. Most shops close on Sundays except in resort areas.

Traditional worry-beads (*komboloi*) make cheap and cheerful souvenirs

Antiquities and Imitations

Genuine antiques and icons require an export permit (rarely granted), and in any case are very thin on the ground. Beware of fakes. The major archaeological museums license a range of accurate and attractive replicas of ancient statues, vases, jewellery and other finds. These are a much better buy.

Beads and Bangles

Brightly coloured ceramic beads, necklaces, gold and silver-plated bracelets, and the black and blue glass beads traditionally believed to ward off the evil eye make cheap and cheerful gifts. *Komboloi* or 'worry-beads', carried by many Greek men, are sold very cheaply in souvenir stores and at every street kiosk.

Clothing

Good buys include cotton sweaters. Thessaloníki, a centre of textile manufacturing, is the cheapest place in Europe for leading-brand denim jeans, shirts and jackets.

Flokati Rugs

Huge, shaggy rugs of wool tufted on to a woven backing may be in natural, unbleached wool or dyed in a variety of vivid colours. Still widely used in Greek homes, they are sold throughout the country.

Footwear

Boots and shoes are well made and affordable. The best buys are to be found in main-street stores where Greeks shop. The sandals sold in tourist markets rarely wear well.

Herbs

Oregano, marjoram and thyme are among the better-known varieties, and prices are much lower than in your supermarket at home. Herbal teas are also widely sold in produce markets.

Jewellery

Jewellers abound, in smaller provincial capitals as well as in Athens, selling gold and silver jewellery based on ancient designs or on more modern interpretations. Prices reflect the value of the material, and while silverware may be cheaper than elsewhere in Europe, gold can be more expensive. Craftsmen in Ioánnina still make silver filigree work, sometimes decorated with turquoise. Antique silver buckles and belts can sometimes be found, but there is no guarantee of authenticity.

Leather Goods

Leather handbags, satchels and travelling bags made solely for the tourist market are sold in markets everywhere. Prices are low and get lower with bargaining, but workmanship is not always first rate. Examine seams, straps and buckles before buying.

Museum Shops

The official shops at major museums sell fine copies of ancient works. They cost more than the poorer imitations sold in tourist shops, but are much better value.

Tax-free Shopping

Value added tax at 18 per cent is charged on anything you buy. Tax-free shopping is available to visitors from outside the European Union at selected shops in Athens and other major cities and resorts. A full list of shops offering VAT refunds to non-EU residents is available from: **Tax Free Club**, Customer Service Office, Syngrou 312, 176 73 Athens; *tel: (210) 957 7091.*

Textiles and Traditional Handicrafts

Woven wool bags, blankets and rugs in bright colours, fine cotton embroidery and lace are among the best souvenirs you can buy. The National Welfare Association's handicraft programme, aimed at keeping Greek traditions alive, provides up to 5,000 women with equipment, designs and raw materials and sells their work through shops in Athens and elsewhere.
National Welfare Association, PO Box 1094, 10110 Athens. Tel: (210) 325 0524.

ATHENS

Adhrianoú, which runs in a crescent through the Plaka, offers gift-hunters a rich choice of ceramics, T-shirts, scarves, hats, sweaters and leather goods made for the visiting shopper. Smart Athenians shop for clothes, shoes, jewellery and accessories elsewhere. The main downtown shopping areas are around Syntagma and Omonia, and in fashionable Kolonaki.

Similar types of stores still tend to cluster together, oriental-style, on the same streets, so you will find a big choice of jewellers' stores on Voukourestiou and around the corner on Venizelou. There are more jewellers on Mitropoleos, which runs west from Syntagma and this is also a good place to look for clothes, shoes and rugs.

Books
Eleftheroudakis

Largest bookshop in town – seven floors, one devoted to English language books. Also has a pleasant café.
Nikis 25, Syntagma. Tel: (210) 322 1401.

The Booknest

Good range of imported books, including English, French, Italian, German and Spanish publications.
Panepistimou 25–29. Tel: (210) 323 1703.

The Kolonaki district offers the smartest shopping in Athens

Flokati Rugs
Gallery Manokali
Traditional flokati rugs.
Kalogrioni 4, Palka. Tel: (210) 324 6785.
Tradition
Handmade carpets and antiques.
Kalogrioni 5, Palka. Tel: (210) 3224 506.

Handicrafts
Kentro Ellinikis Paradosis
(Centre of Hellenic Tradition)
Hidden away in an arcade you will find
this delightful store stocking quality
Greek folk art, paintings, wood-
carvings, ceramics, icons and
embroidery. There's also a charming café
with a view of the Acropolis.
Metropoleos 59 and Pandrossou 36,
Plaka. Tel: (210) 3213 023.

National Welfare Organization
Shops sell handwoven rugs, embroidery,
lace and other arts and crafts from all
over Greece.
Voukourestiou 24, Ipatias 6 (inside the
Hilton) and Vasilissis Sofias 46.
Tel: (210) 325 0524.

Jewellery
Agora Ethnic
Reasonably priced handmade ethnic
necklaces, bracelets and earrings, using a
remix of old beads and semi-precious
stones.
Pandrossou 10, Plaka.
Tel: (210) 3248 247.
Lalaounis
Designs in gold and silver based on
ancient motifs.
Panepistimiou 6 and Voukourestiou 12.
Tel: (210) 361 1371.
Zolotas
With Lalaounis, the best-known of the
Athens gold and silver sellers.
Panepistimiou 10. Tel: (210) 3613 782.

Museum Shops
Mousio Benaki (Benaki Museum)
Greek handicrafts, textiles and jewellery.
A good place to shop for gifts.
Koumbari 1. Tel: (210) 367 1000.
Mousio Ethniko Arkheologiko
(National Archaeological Museum)
Copies of many of the museum's finest
exhibits.
Patission 44. Tel: (210) 821 7717.
Mousio Goulandri Kykladhiki Texni
(Goulandris Museum of Cycladic Art)
Accurate copies of the marvellous 5,000-
year-old Cycladic figurines.
Neofytou Douka 4.
Tel: (210) 724 9706.

Shoes
Look for branches of the city-wide Kalogirou or Mocassino chains in main shopping areas.

Music
Virgin Megastore
Biggest selection of music in town, including a large section devoted to traditional Greek tunes.
Stadiou 7-9, Syntagma.
Tel: (210) 3314 788.

Markets
Ifaistou (Ifestou)
The original venerable Flea Market on Ifestou is a mixture of trendy clothes and shoe-stores, and glory-holes where you can buy anything from a postman's battered leather satchel to an army surplus parachute or a World War I artillery shell crafted into a beaten-brass flower vase. One long-established shop has a line in helmets which ranges from copies of those worn at the Battle of Marathón in 490 BC to German and Italian headgear from World War II.

Another sells antique prams, toys and carved animals from fairground carousels. The Flea Market is also a good place to buy hiking and camping gear. The best day to visit is Sunday, when the market spills over into surrounding streets and becomes a happy hunting ground for bargain-seeking Athenians.
Next to Monastiráki metro station.
Kendrikí Agorá (Central Market)
The Kendrikí Agorá (Central Market) is a photographer's heaven, though the squeamish may find the meat market section, with its racks of carcases and innards, a bit hard to take. The fish market, with stall after stall selling seafood from tiny whitebait to huge grouper and tunny, is spectacular. In surrounding streets are shops and stalls selling dried herbs and nuts, sweets, fruit, vegetables, game and household goods.

The market cafés in the pre-dawn hours are a favourite rendezvous for Athenian nightlifers who have outlasted the city's bars and clubs. The market opens at first light.
10 minutes' walk from Monastiraki metro station, on the corner of Athinas and Evripidou.
Pandrosou (Pandhrossou)
Both sides of Pandhrossou are packed with shops selling smart leatherwear, fashion jewellery and replica antiques, and there is not a flea in sight. Most of the new shops take major credit cards.

AROUND GREECE
Away from Athens and the main holiday resorts, the stalls of the *laiki* (popular) market, where local people shop for fruit, vegetables and household supplies, are great places to shop and wander. The *laiki* is usually held several mornings a week in a main square or street. You can find out when and where at the local *dhimarkion* (town hall) or police station. Bargains include linen and embroidery, enamelled pots and pans, tiny coffee cups and, in recent years, Russian-made watches, cameras and binoculars peddled by Greek refugees from the former USSR.

Village hardware stores, usually on or near the market square, are great places for souvenirs such as hammered brass

New and old designs are replicated in gold and silver

and copper trays, goat-bells, striped blankets or walking sticks.

Several Greek towns have a special reputation for locally made products. Arákhova is known for its wool rugs, Ioánnina for its silverware and Kastoría for its patchwork furs. Here and elsewhere, one shop is much the same as its neighbour and a walk down the main street will give you a good idea of what is for sale and how much it costs. Prices will be much the same around town. Bargaining is common, but do not expect to beat the asking price down by more than about 10 per cent. Cash always commands lower prices than credit cards.

Arákhova

Coarsely-woven wool rugs and blankets dyed in earthy reds, orange and black are made locally and sold in stores along the main street, along with shepherds' twisty staffs and carved olive-wood kitchen ware.

Delphi

Modern Delphi's two main streets are packed with shops selling replicas from this and other archaeological excavations. Quality varies. The best bear the seal of approval of the National Archaeological Museum in Athens.

Ioánnina

A delightfully ramshackle bazaar area of medieval-looking workshops and stores lies just inland from Dionysou Filosofotou and the walled old town. For Ioánnina's famous silver filigree, visit the many jewellers' shops on Nissia, the island just offshore.

Kastoría

The lakeside city has been famous for its furriers for more than 2,000 years. Their speciality is piecing together garments from scraps of fur, and most of their work can be bought as cheaply in Athens as from the workshops here. Beware, too, of buying garments made from the fur of endangered species. Though technically illegal, this trade continues to flourish. Buyers can be fined and their purchases confiscated by Customs on their return home.

Komotiní

An old-fashioned maze of streets northeast of Platia Ireni, the main square, houses a picturesque bazaar area and a bustling arcaded produce market. The antique shops along Venizelou, the pedestrianised main artery of the quarter, are piled with antique, inlaid furniture, Turkish hookahs, lamps and candlesticks – as well as plenty of fakes.

Olympia

Museum Art of Greece is worth the investment for its outstanding replicas of statues and bronzes and also for its fine reproductions of Byzantine icons. *Leoforos Kondhili 15. Tel: (262) 402 2573.*

Thessaloníki

Thessaloníki's bazaar area – a rectangle bounded by Egnatias, Dhragoumi, Aristotelous and Tsimiski – offers the best street shopping in Greece. It is also a great place for photography, with stalls selling everything from live fish to fake designer watches. Look for these and other bargains on Venizelou and Ermou, or for colourful stalls selling fruit, vegetables, meat and seafood in the huge central market.

The Thessaloníki Archaeological Museum shop sells excellent replicas of exhibits and antiquities from this and other Greek museums.

Fresh farm produce sold cheaply at a makeshift counter

Entertainment

Entertainment in Greece embraces everything from the tragedies of Sophocles to the traditional music and dances of rural Greece, which are performed not only for tourists but for the Greeks' own enjoyment. In Athens, several English-language newspapers and magazines (daily, weekly and monthly) have entertainment pages which list current performances. The most reliable is *Athens News* (daily). Elsewhere, your best bet is the local tourist office (*see p189*), the *dhimarkion* (town hall) or, in holiday resorts, a travel and ticket agency.

The National Theatre at Athens

Cinemas
In major cities you can catch recently released US and European films, with Greek subtitles. Many local cinemas in smaller towns have closed down.

ATHENS
Indoor Cinema
Asty
Korai 4, off Panepistimou.
Tel: (210) 322 1925.
Athina
Patission 122. Tel: (210) 823 3149
Atlantis
Vouliagmenis 245. Tel: (210) 971 1511.
Elli
Akadimias 64. Tel: (210) 363 2789.
Plaza
Kifissias 118. Tel: (210) 692 1667

Open-air Summer Cinema
Alexandra
Patission 77–79. Tel: (210) 821 9298
Cine Pallini
Venizelou 3 and Marathonos Aveneu.
Tel: (210) 666 6815.

Cine Pari
Kydathinaion 22, Plaka.
Tel: (210) 322 2071 .
Riviera
Valtetsiou 46, Exarchia.
Tel: (210) 383 7716.
Thission
Pavlou 7, Thissio. Tel: (210) 347 0980

THESSALONÍKI
Indoor Cinema
Alexandros
Ethnikis Aminis 1. Tel: (230) 125 7255.
Esperos
SvoUlou 2. Tel: (230) 1235 304.
Macedonikon
Filikis Etarias 44. Tel: (230)126 1727.
Pallas
Leoforos Nikis 73. Tel: (230) 127 8515.

Open-air Summer Cinema
Natali
Paralai-Stratigio. Tel: (230) 182 9457.

Classical Music
Concerts and performances are held

frequently in both Thessaloníki and Athens.

ATHENS

Athens Concert Hall (Mégaron Mousikis Athenon)
Leofóros Vassilissis Sofias.
Tel: (210) 728 2333; www.megaron.gr
Olympia Theatre
Akadimias 59–61.
Tel: (210) 361 2461;
www.nationalopera.gr
Hellenic American Union
Massalias 22. Tel: (210) 368 0000;
www.hau.gr

THESSALONÍKI

Kratiko Theatro (Odhos Pavlou Mela)
Tel: (230) 122 3785.
Thessaloníki Concert Hall
25th Martiou and Paralath Martiou.
Tel: (231) 089 5800; www.tch.gr

Cultural Events

Annual drama festivals are held regularly which both preserve Greece's ancient dramatic heritage and encourage modern productions and interpretations of the classical playwrights.

If you have an interest in classical drama or in modern music, opera, ballet and dance you should not miss the Athens and Epídhavros Festivals which are held simultaneously every year from mid-June to the end of September. Exact dates may be checked by logging on to *www.cultureguide.gr* or from the Greek National Tourist Office (*see p189*).

ATHENS

Spread from mid-June to late September is the annual **Athens Festival.**

Contact: The Hellenic Festival Box Office, Panepistimiou 39.
Tel: (210) 322 1459; www.greekfestival.gr

EPÍDHAVROS

The annual **Epídhavros Festival** features performances of classical plays from the 5th century BC in the ancient Theatre of Epídhavros (mid–Jun–mid–Sep).
Hellenic Festival Box Office in Athens.

IOÁNNINA

The **Ioánnina Festival** of classical and modern theatre, and traditional dance from June to September at the ancient theatre at Dhodhóni.
Tel: (265) 102 0090.

KAVÁLLA

Festival of Philippi shows classical drama in the theatre at Filippi (Philippi) and on the island of Thásos from July to September.
Tel: (251) 022 3504.

PATRAS

The annual Patras Festival held from June to September combines jazz, classical music and theatre.
Tel: (261) 027 5272.

THESSALONÍKI

Thessaloniki Film Festival
International festival held since 1992
(www.filmfestival.gr).

Dimitria Festival
Held from September to December and features classical and modern drama, music, ballet and opera performed by Greek and foreign companies.
Tel: (231) 028 1068.

Music

Traditional Greek music is a mix of eastern and western influences. Greeks are fond of modern pop, but the wailing minor keys and unfamiliar rhythms of their own songs and dances have a strong flavour of the older, more oriental Greece. The most familiar music to visitors – played for the dance you are most likely to be invited to join – is the *sirtos*, a follow-my-leader circle-dance for any number of dancers. Typical instruments all over Greece include guitar, lute, fiddle and tambourine, with or without the accompaniment of various wind instruments typical of each region.

Bouzouki or rembetika music was brought to Athens by Greek refugees from Turkey in the 1920s and became fashionable among wealthy Athenians, who would ostentatiously applaud the musicians by smashing their dinner-plates. The surviving *bouzouki* clubs of Athens are expensive and only for real enthusiasts. If you go, remember that smashing the crockery is an expensive kind of applause – you have to pay for the breakages.

Traditional ballads often recall the heroes of the epic struggle to throw off the Turkish yoke and many dances are re-enactments of historic incidents. In the north, these ballads include the mournful *kleftiko* of Epirus, celebrating the deeds of the *klefts*, mountain bandits who, like Robin Hood, are also remembered as heroes of the national resistance.

The music of Thrace and Macedonia features a number of unique wind instruments, including the *gaida*, a local version of the bagpipe, a shrill oboe called the *zournas*, and a type of flute called the *kaval*. Unlike the stately circles of Epirus, the regional dances are rapid and energetic, with much fancy footwork.

The typical folk music of the Peloponnese is the lively *palea dhimotika* ballad, driven along by guitar, fiddle and tambourine and recounting tales of daring, victory and defeat.

Music is integral to social life all over Greece and renderings of traditional folksongs as well as contemporary hits liven many an evening

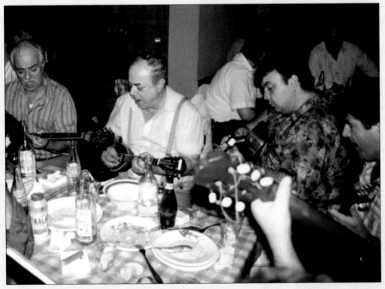

Dancing

Dancing is a part of any celebration, even the most impromptu, for Greeks are still very much in the habit of making their own amusement.

Even among the fashionable youth of Greece, an evening spent dancing to the latest electronic beat may well end in the small hours with a traditional *sirtos*.

You can sample an evening of the kind of traditional entertainment Greeks enjoy at any *exoxiko kentro* (country centre). These are usually some kilometres from the nearest town, offering city-dwelling Greeks a nostalgic evening of home cooking, wine from the barrel, powerfully amplified traditional music, and dancing – both by performers and the audience.

One of the best places to sample Greek music and dance is at the **Dora Stratou Dance Centre** *Théatro on Filopapou in Athens. Tel: (210) 3244 395.* The late Dora Stratou was single-handedly responsible for saving much of Greece's musical heritage. She recorded many tunes and dances which had never been written down and were in danger of vanishing with the generation of villagers who remembered them. Her work rekindled interest in folk music, and the Dora Stratou troupes perform dances from all over the mainland and islands, not only at their own open-air theatre in Athens but at festivals throughout Greece and worldwide. The theatre is open nightly from May to September. Tickets are usually available on the night of the performance, or can be booked through agencies, main hotels, or from the theatre.

Discos

Tourism has combined with the Greek love of any kind of dancing to ensure that every holiday resort has an oversupply of discos and dance clubs. These start to warm up around midnight, play the latest dance hits at maximum volume and change name, ownership and venue virtually every season. Many are no more than an open-air dance floor, bar and sound system overlooking the beach. There is little to choose among them – pick whichever nightspot takes your fancy. Admission to clubs and discos is usually free, but drinks are more expensive than in an ordinary bar. Bigger indoor clubs with the usual lasers, dry ice and dance music can be found in Athens, but most of them close during the summer, when their DJs and many of their clientele head for the bright lights of the islands.

ATHENS

Decadence

Students come here to dance to alternative rock and retro music. *Voulgaroktonou 69 (Exarhia).*

Folio

Reggae, funk and Latin in this club. *Eslin 4 (Ambelokipi),.*

Greek women traditionally wore elaborately embroidered costumes and magnificent necklaces to dance on feast days and at weddings

Greek dancers in traditional costumes at the Dora Stratou Dance Centre

Neon
A large, modern bar-nightclub with tables outside overlooking the water close to Mikrolimano.
Akti Dilaveri 5 (Piraeus).

Privilege
Athen's most exclusive club, frequented by the rich and famous. Moves to the coast in summer.
Ag Eleoussis and Kakourgodikou (Monastiraki).

Plus Soda
Some of Europe's top DJ's come to play here. Moves to the coast in summer.
Ermou 161 (Thissio).

Rodon
Live rock concerts in a converted cinema in the city centre.
Marni 24 (Omonia).

U-Mati
Dance music and occasional live concerts.
Vouliagmeni 268 (Vouliagmeni)

Venue
House and techno predominate in this chic and trendy club.
L Kifoias 101 (Marousi).

Television and Video

The television is a fixture in every small rural *kafeneon* or *tavérna*. The national TV channels ET1 and ET2 broadcast a steady diet of imported British and US films, programmes and soap operas which are subtitled in Greek. Satellite TV is spreading fast and is offered by most business hotels and many larger resort hotels.

Many hotels and bars in the more popular international holiday resorts also offer a nightly programme of video movies, sports and music programmes from around the world. There is no charge for these – the idea is to lure you into the bar.

Café Society

The Greek café has undergone a quiet revolution in recent years. It is still the mainstay of local nightlife, but it is no longer restricted to older men. In most towns and villages the evening starts with the *volta*, a twilight stroll along the waterfront or around the *platia* by old and young – from wizened patriarchs and proud grannies showing off their latest grandchildren to dapper teenage dandies eyeing potential partners. Then the generations separate. Older women return home while their husbands settle down for an evening in a favourite old-style *kafeneon* to drink ouzo or coffee and talk politics over cards or backgammon. Meanwhile, the younger generation

will hop from one bright new café-bar to the next. Bar-hopping can mean no more than moving to the next table – most cafés huddle together by the harbour or around the main square, and it takes an educated eye to figure out which outdoor tables belong to which bar. Owners of these glossy establishments favour exotic names like Apocalypse, Bikini Red, Tequila Sunrise or No Name. An equally exotic selection of fancy imported liquor is always proudly on display behind the gleaming bar, but young Greeks are as likely to drink iced coffee – which is just as well, since the motorcycle is their favoured transport. And although the old *kafeneon* is traditionally an exclusively male domain, younger Greek women (like their boyfriends) head for the café-bars to see and be seen.

Café society: old and new

Children

Greece welcomes children warmly and there are very few places anywhere where they cannot be taken. Couples will frequently be cross-examined as to whether or not they have children and if not, why not? Greeks regard children as an unmixed blessing, and crying babies or the fractious late-night behaviour of tired youngsters will be tolerated in village *tavérnas* and cafés.

Greek youngsters have the run of the village and the *tavérna*

Food
Food should not be a problem, even if your children are picky eaters who insist on a chips-only diet. These are on every Greek menu, as are other plain and familiar dishes such as fish, burgers, and salad. Canned soft drinks are universally available, as are most well-known brands of sweets and chocolate bars, ice-cream and ice lollies. Sticky Greek cakes and desserts from the *zacharoplasteion* (pastry shop) are also a hit with young children.

Greece is above all a country where life is lived outdoors almost all year round, and Greek youngsters are raised on a free-range basis with the whole village and its surroundings as a playground. Visiting toddlers can easily join in.

The Seaside
The main attraction for families visiting Greece is the beach, and sea and sand are the focus of most family resorts. Greece's seas have little or no tide, so the sea is always at your doorstep and is almost always calm enough even for young children to swim in safety.

Sheltered, gently-shelving sandy beaches ideal for families with small children can be found on the Khalkidhikí (Chalkidiki) peninsulas in Macedonia (*see pp122–3*), in the southern Peloponnese at Koróni and Methóni (*see pp64–5*) and Stoupa (*see p77*), and in Argolis at Tolón (*see p58*).

Things to Do
Children with an interest in wild flowers and wildlife will find Greece a delight, with dozens of birds, lizards, tortoises and turtles, butterflies and other insects to identify and watch. Those with an interest in marine life will find the clear waters of inlets and harbours as full of sea creatures as any marine aquarium, and will be fascinated by the varied haul unloaded by fishing boats each morning. The end of any Greek village pier always attracts a gaggle of junior anglers, and simple hook-and-line kits are sold in all village shops.

Pedaloes, canoes, and other simple watersports equipment are for hire at all summer beach resorts, and older children can use them with confidence in shallow waters and enclosed coves. Although Greek waters have virtually no tides, they do have inshore currents so caution must be used. Bicycles for children and adults can also be rented at some resorts.

Children with an interest in history will find that the ancient sites, medieval castles and deserted fortresses of mainland Greece offer a fascinating 'hands-on' lesson in the past, and younger children will enjoy scrambling to the highest tiers of the ancient theatres. Running races in the millennia-old stadium at Olympia or Delphi can be a welcome release of energy after the journey. In the unlikely event of poor weather, a visit to one of the many folklore museums with their displays of traditional costumes, kitchenware, tools, weapons and jewellery will keep children entertained.

Purpose-built facilities and entertainment for children are rarely provided. Most villages have a small playground, though old-fashioned wood and metal swings and roundabouts are

The National Gardens in Athens offer an escape from city traffic for children and parents

potential hazards for smaller children. Some larger resorts and hotels have separate swimming pools for toddlers, and many package tour operators offer fun-clubs, child-minding and babysitting services (*see p181*).

Sheltered beaches and seas with little tidal variation allow children hours of pleasure

Sport and Leisure

The great sporting passions of Greece are basketball and soccer, which are watched avidly both live and on television and are enthusiastically played at all levels. It is a small village indeed which does not have a dusty football pitch on its outskirts and a basketball pitch in its schoolyard or outside the village hall.

Basketball has become a national passion, rivalling football

Though not traditionally the nation's favourite, Basketball has outstripped soccer in the popularity stakes. This was partly because of the Greek national team which performs strongly in international events. However, in 1994 the Greek soccer team succeded in qualifying for the World Cup in the USA. This rekindled the popular enthusiasm for soccer. Today, graffiti acclaiming the top Athenian team, Panathinaikos (PAO), can be seen not only in Athens but all over the country.

The most important national venue for football and other sporting events is the Peace and Friendship Stadium (Nea Faliron, Athens; *tel: (210) 481 9513*).

Basketball
Greek Basketball Federation
N Saripolou 11, Athens.
Tel: (210) 824 4125; www.basket.gr

Soccer
Matches are regularly played on Sundays at 5.30pm in season, which lasts from October to April. Tickets are available at each team office.
Greek Soccer Federation
Syngrou 137, Athens. Tel: (210) 9336 410;
www.epo.gr

SPORTS FOR VISITORS
Golf
Greece has the ideal climate for golf, especially in spring and autumn, but there are only two courses on the mainland which approach international standards.
Glyfadha Golf Club
The only high-quality golf course in Greece is in the seaside suburb of Glifádha (Glyfadha). It offers an 18-hole course, dressing rooms, sports store, restaurant and bar.
Kyros/15 Panopis, Glyfada, signposted.
12km from central Athens.
Tel: (210) 8946 820.
Porto Carras
This is a resort complex that includes an 18-hole course.
Khalkidhikí. Tel: 23750 71221;
www.portocarras.com

Running
The heroic first Marathon run (*see p50*) is re-enacted twice a year, for seeded athletes in April and for all runners in October.
SEGAS (Greek Sports and Athletics Federation
Syngrou 137, Athens. Tel: (210) 935 9346;
www.segas.gr

Skiing

Skiing is increasingly popular in Greece, and although Greek slopes do not rank with the best in Europe they are certainly among the cheapest. The ski season begins in mid-December and continues until the end of April, when you can combine a day's skiing with a holiday on the beach or touring. The main ski centres are at Kalavrita, near Patras (*see p83*) Parnassós, near Delphi (*see p86 & pp96–7*) and on Pélion (*see pp112–13*).

Kalavrita Ski Centre
Tel: (269) 202 2174.

Parnassós Ski Centre
24km from Arákhova. Tel: (223) 402 2689; www.parnassos-eot.gr

Pelion Ski Centre
27km from Vólos. Tel: 24210 99136.

Tennis

There are tennis courts on a number of the beaches and resorts managed by the Greek National Tourist Office

EFOA (Greek Tennis Association), Omirou 8, Athens; *tel: (210) 323 0412.*

Athens Tennis Club
Vasilissis Olgas, Athens.
Tel: (210) 923 2872.

Yachting

Yachts of all sizes are available for charter from Greek marinas, with or without skipper and crew. With hundreds of coves and beaches, islets and hideaway harbours accessible only by sea, Greece is the best yachting country in the Mediterranean. A list of yacht charterers is available from the Greek National Tourist Office (*see p189*).

Hellenic Sailing Federation
Akti Navarchou Kountouioti, Kastella, Piraeus. Tel: (210) 323 5560.

Yacht Club of Athens
Karageorgis Servias, Mikrolimano, Piraeus. Tel: (210) 417 1823.

Naval Club of Thessaloníki
Themistokli Sofouli 112.
Tel: (231) 042 9777.

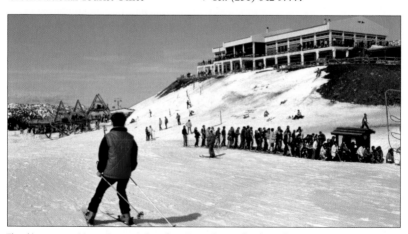

The ski season on Mount Parnassós lasts from December until early April

Waterskiing

Waterskiing facilities are available at all holiday beaches in summer and there are waterski schools at most major resorts. Contact the **Greek Waterskiing Association** (Possidonos, Agios Kosmas, Athens; *tel: (210) 894 7413, www. waterski.org.gr*).

Windsurfing

Greece's waters, with their reliable breezes, are perfect for windsurfing and boards are for hire at every beach resort. A number of international events are held each year. For details, contact the Greek National Tourist Office (*see p189*).

ADVENTURE SPORTS

Greece's mountain landscapes are an adventure playground offering an exciting and extensive range of activities.

Greek waters provide perfect conditions for windsurfing

Caving

The limestone rock of mainland Greece is riddled with long cave systems and underground lakes and rivers. Many of these have been opened up to visitors under the management of the Greek National Tourist Office, but kilometres of caverns still remain to be explored.
Hellenic Speleological Society
Sina 32, Athens. Tel: (210) 361 7824.

Climbing and Trekking

Greece's mountains are wonderful for walkers, offering relatively gentle routes which can be completed in one or two days as well as much more demanding itineraries. Mount Olympus, the highest mountain in Greece and the second highest in the Balkan region, is a surprisingly undemanding ascent and from May to mid-October is within the abilities of most reasonably fit walkers, with well-marked trails and dormitory accommodation in several mountain refuges (*see p140*). Another relatively easy trek, which can be completed in one day, takes you to Drakolimin, a mountain lake on the slopes of Tímfi Óros (Mount Timfi) in the Píndhos range; the spectacular Vikos Gorge in the same region, offers a demanding one (*see pp110–11*) In southern Greece, the ascent to Profitis Ilias, the highest peak of the Taïyetos range, is still more demanding. The Greek Alpine Club, which manages refuges on all these mountains, publishes a range of guides and detailed route maps and can advise on mountain conditions, equipment and when to go.

Rock climbing is growing in popularity, but the soft, crumbly limestone of most Greek mountains is not ideal climbing rock, attractive though it looks.

Basic mountain safety rules must be obeyed even on shorter walks, as the mountains are thinly populated and a sprained ankle far from help can spell disaster. Take plenty of water, and make sure that someone knows where you are going and when you expect to be back. Nights on the higher slopes are chilly even in high summer, and you will need proper walking boots – not just trainers – for more serious trekking. Other essentials include a water-bottle and water sterilising tablets.

EOS (Greek Alpine Club) maintains refuges with dormitories on the main trekking routes. On Olympus, these are staffed and serve simple meals. Elsewhere, they are usually unstaffed and you must get the key from the local EOS office in the nearest village. The EOS also supplies information, bulletins and maps.

Ellinikos Orivatikos Sindhesmos (EOS)
Hellenic Federation of Mountainering & Climbing.
Milioni 5, Athens. Tel: (210) 364 5904.

Hang-gliding

The bright-coloured delta wings of hang-gliders can often be seen circling over the steep ridges of the Píndhos mountains near Ioánnina (*see pp104–5*) which create great up-draughts.

Scuba Diving

Until recently the Greek authorities have held diving in deep suspicion, fearing the theft of antiquities from seabed sites. Key underwater archaeological sites have

A rock climber pits his skill against the pinnacles and precipices of the Metéora

now been thoroughly mapped and remain off-limits, but you can learn to dive at Vouliagméni and at Várkiza, near Athens (*see p47*) and there is more extensive diving off the coast of Sidhonia (*see pp122–3*). Rules for divers are strict and include a ban on touching, removing or even photographing any antiquities you find and on spear-fishing with scuba gear. Visibility in Greek waters is usually excellent, but there is less underwater life than you might expect – the result of thousands of years of intensive fishing.

Hellenic Federation of Underwater Activities
Agios Kosmas, West Terminal Post Office. Athens. Tel: (210) 981 9961.

Ancient Olympic Games

The Olympic Games, first recorded in 776 BC, were staged on the plains of Olympia and dedicated to the God of Gods, Zeus. They lasted one day and featured running and wrestling. In 472 BC, the event was extended to five days, with the addition of boxing, the pancration (a cross between boxing and wrestling), horse-racing and the pentathlon (comprising sprint, long-jump, javelin, discus and wrestling). The games were held every four years, and an Olympic truce was declared for their duration to protect travelling athletes and spectators. Competitors arrived from all corners of the ancient Greek world to compete for the first prize – an olive wreath – and to uphold the Olympic values of noble competition and effort to combine body, spirit and mind as a balanced whole. Women were not admitted to the games, either as competitors or spectators. The Olympics were banned in AD 393 by Emperor Theodosius who considered them pagan.

Modern Olympic Games

The Olympic Games were revived by the French Baron Pierre de Coubertin in 1896, and staged in the renovated 4th century BC Panathinaikon Stadium in Athens. Just over 200 men representing 14 countries competed in 43 events. The first prize was a silver medal, a certificate and an olive wreath. Women first competed in the games in Paris in 1900, though they only made up about 20 of the total 1000 competitors from 28 countries. Worldwide spectator participation was made possible in 1960 when the Games were televised for the first time from Rome.

The modern Olympics have been held continually every four years since 1896, apart from during the two World Wars.

The Goal of the Olympic Movement

According to the Olympic Charter, established by Pierre de Coubertin, the goal of the Olympic Movement is to contribute to building a peaceful and better world by educating youth through sport practiced without discrimination of any kind and in the Olympic spirit, which requires mutual understanding with a spirit of friendship, solidarity and fair play.

Unfortunately, today boycotts and terrorism have crept in increasingly to dilute and threaten this apolitical spirit of the games.

Athens 2004

In 2004, from 13–29 August, Athens
will once again host the Olympic
Games. 199 countries will be eligible to
compete in 28 sports events. The main
venue will be the Athens Olympic Sports
Complex on Kifissias Avenue, in the
northern suburb of Maroussi. Although
the stadium was originally built in 1982,
it is currently being expanded and will
host the opening and closing
ceremonies, in addition to a number of
events. The old marble Panathinaikon
Stadium in the city centre will host
archery and the marathon finish. Greeks
will be hoping for their best results in
weightlifting, in which they won five
medals in Sydney in 2000.

For further information check out the
website: *www.athens2004.com.*

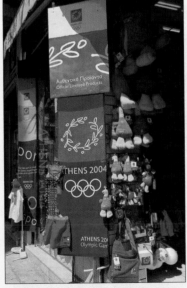

Posters and souvenirs designed for the 2004
Olympic Games

Food and Drink

The best Greek food is the simplest: fish straight from the boat, vegetables fresh from the field served as salad with wild herbs and olives or in stews. Most restaurants offer multilingual menus. The translations can be as opaque as the original Greek, inviting you to sample 'smashed bowels in roasted spit' or 'one brain salad'. Puzzling them out is half the fun ('one brain salad' is just that – a sheep's brain served cold atop a bed of lettuce).

Fresh fish is always on the menu in Greek harbour towns and holiday resorts

You will sometimes be invited into the kitchen to choose your meal, while in the smallest restaurants you just take pot luck or make do with omelettes, chips and salad. Only in the smartest restaurants will food be served course by course.

Mezé, a selection of dishes served simultaneously, is a Greek culinary tradition, and in smaller restaurants everything often comes at once or in an unexpected order – chips, for example, often arrive first as a kind of appetiser.

A display of traditional bottled foods

Fish

Fish is priced according to weight and category. You choose your fish from the kitchen, where it is then weighed and the price calculated before filleting. Seafood is popular but pricey, with delicacies like *barboúnia* (red mullet) and *melanouryia* (no translation) at the top of the price range. Swordfish (*xifías*) steaks are always available and moderately priced, usually coming in enormous portions. At the cheaper end of the scale are *marídes* (whitebait), *goúpes* (sprats) and *kalamáres* (fried baby squid). *Astakós* (langouste, though usually translated as lobster) is expensive by local standards, though most visitors will think it good value. Unfamiliar seafood dishes include *oktapódhi* (octopus) served in a variety of ways, either cold as a snack, grilled, or in a stew with rice or pasta.

In northern Greece, with its many lakes, you will find freshwater fish like carp and eel on the menu along with crayfish, lake crabs and frogs' legs.

Meat Dishes

Moussaká (lamb or veal cooked in layers of cheese and aubergine), *yiouvétsi* (beef stewed with noodles in a clay pot), *kotópoulo* (roast or grilled chicken) and *souvláki* (veal, lamb or pork cooked on a skewer) appears on most menus. In the north, a spicy sausage called *spetsofaí* is often served in a stew with vegetables. More familiar meat dishes include grilled lamb chops or pork cutlets, and *keftédhes* (meat balls in sauce). Chips are the favoured accompaniment to meat dishes.

Vegetable Dishes

The 'traditional' Greek salad is a meal in itself, featuring heaps of tomatoes,

A slab of strong-flavoured *feta* cheese is the heart of a Greek salad

onion, cucumber, green peppers, and olives drowned in oil and flavoured with dried herbs. It is known as *horiatikí* only in tourist restaurants, where it is usually served crowned with feta cheese (if you don't want cheese, ask for *salata hores feta*, salad without cheese).

FOOD AND DRINK			
food	fagito	skewered meat	souvlakia
bread	psomi	pork	chirini
water	nero	spinach	spanaki
wine	krasi	courgette	kolokithia
beer	bira	beans	fasoles
coffee	kafes	chips	patates tiganites
lobster	astakos	cucumber	angouri
squid	kalamares/kalamarakia	tomato	tomata
otopus	oktapodhi	olives	elies
red mullet	barbounia	salad with feta	horiatiki
whitebait	maridhes	tomato salad	salata
lamb	arni	yoghurt and	tsatsiki
chicken	kotopoulo	cucumber dip	
meat balls	keftedhes		

Octopus is a Greek favourite but an acquired taste for visitors

Dishes like *gemistá* (tomatoes or green peppers stuffed with herb-flavoured rice) and *dolmádes* (stuffed vine leaves) may or may not contain meat. Vegetable-only dishes include *vriam* (ratatouille), and a variety of pulses including *fakes* (lentil stew), *gigantes* (stewed broad beans), *mavromati* (boiled black-eye beans served cold with coriander) and *fasolákia* (green beans stewed with tomatoes). Cold dishes include *tsatsíki* (yoghurt flavoured with cucumber and garlic).

PLACES TO EAT AND DRINK

Greeks eat late, and dinner is the big meal of the day. In resorts where tourists outnumber locals, restaurants have adjusted to the foreign habit of eating early in the evening. If your first choice of restaurant is full, you will almost always find others, just as good, next door or near by. Dress codes are virtually non-existent for both men and women; generally, a clean shirt for men and anything other than beachwear for women is acceptable anywhere and most outdoor resort restaurants are accustomed to serving daytime clients in bathing suits.

Greek eating-places fall into a number of categories. Virtually all serve alcohol at all times (except on election day) but some offer a full menu, others only snacks, pot luck, or specialities. Most restaurants stay open late – Greeks set on a night out will dine at 10pm, stay till after midnight, then go on to a bar or nightclub. In summer, almost all dining is alfresco, except in major cities.

Bars

Places described as bars or 'pubs' are usually smart, shiny and relatively expensive, serving cocktails and imported liquors and beers to a younger clientele and often open only after dark. In busier resorts, an early-evening 'happy hour' often attracts a noisy clientele. Bars usually serve only soft drinks, alcohol and iced coffee.

Estiatórion (Restaurant)

Open for lunch and dinner, the *estiatórion* is where Greeks go on family occasions. In major cities, restaurants can be quite formal but in resorts they are usually friendly and relaxed and offer the widest choice of meals and drinks.

Rizokalo (rice pudding flavoured with cinnamon)

Kafenéon

The *kafenéon* is the nearest thing Greece has to a neighbourhood bar or pub. Open all day and usually past midnight, it serves coffee (Greek or instant), Greek spirits, beer and *retsina*, often with a plateful of snacks such as sunflower seeds, cubes of cheese, or slices of sausage. It is a centre of village social life (or in big cities the focus for a block of shops or apartments) and many older men spend much of their day at a café table over tiny cups of coffee or glasses of *ouzo*.

Ouzerí

The *ouzerí* serves *ouzo* (of course), wine, beer and coffee, almost always accompanied by *mezé*, a series of substantial snacks which can add up to a light meal.

Psarotavérna (Fish Restaurant)

The *psarotavérna* specialises in seafood, usually overlooks the harbour and is probably the most expensive place to eat. The menu will include the full gamut of fish and crustaceans, but few alternatives.

Psistariá (Grill Restaurant)

For carnivores only, the *psistariá* serves grilled meat of all kinds. The grill is usually up front, and like the *psarotavérna*, few alternative dishes are offered.

Tavérna

A catch-all term for an unpretentious restaurant where you eat what is in the pot that day, washing it down with jugs of wine, the *tavérna* is to be approached with caution. In out of the way corners of Athens and Thessaloníki there are delightful old *tavérnas* where you can eat the best meal of your Greek holiday at a very affordable price. In busy holiday centres, however, anywhere calling itself a *tavérna* is likely to be a tourist trap pure and simple. As a general rule, if most of your fellow diners are Greeks you are in for a treat; if they are foreigners, think twice.

Zacharoplasteíon (Pastry Shop)

If you have a sweet tooth the *zacharoplasteíon* is the place for you. Selling sweet pastries and sticky cakes to take away or eat at pavement tables, it also serves Greek and instant coffee and soft drinks.

Meze snacks traditionally accompany a mid-morning glass of aniseed-flavoured *ouzo*

Local diners at an old-style *tavérna* in the city of Thessaloníki

Where to Eat

You can eat well in even the smallest of Greek villages. Most of them have more than their fair share of cheap and simple *tavérnas*. In most resorts and country towns there is little to choose between one eating-place and its neighbour, so stroll along the harbour or round the square and pick whichever takes your fancy. Eat where the Greeks eat and you will find the food better, cheaper and more varied than in restaurants catering only to holidaymakers. Few restaurants in Greece are worth a special visit, and those as much for the view or the atmosphere as for the food. We have listed restaurants in Greece's three main cities, as well as a handful of other places which stand out from the crowd.

The following table is an indication of restaurant prices. The ★ sign indicates the cost of a three-course meal for one without wine. A half-litre carafe of *retsina* or beer costs around €3, a bottle of red or white wine between €16–€30. Only the most up-market city restaurants accept telephone reservations. Prices rose steeply with the introduction of the euro in 2002, but now look set to stabilise.

★   under €20
★★   under €30
★★★   under €40
★★★★ over €40

ATHENS

Abyssinia Cafe ★★

A great place to stop for lunch while exploring the Monastiraki market. A tempting selection of meze are served in a wood-panelled dining room overlooking the furniture restorers' workshops.

Kinetou 7, Avisinia Square, Monastiraki.
Tel: (210) 321 7047.

Archeon Gefsis ★★

This highly original restaurant serves up
the sort of dishes the ancient Greeks
would have eaten. Many combine meat,
goat's cheese and wild berries. Tables are
set with a spoon and knife, but no fork.
Kodratou 22, Omonio.
Tel: (210) 523 9661.

Bakalarakia ★

The Athenian version of a fish and chip
restaurant. Specialities include battered
cod and *skordalia*, a dish made with
mashed potatoes, olive oil and garlic.

*Kidathineon 41, Plaka. Tel: (210) 322
5084.Closed: late-May–early-Oct.*

Dafne's ★★★★

This romantic restaurant offers sophis-
icated Greek cuisine in a frescoed dining
room in Plaka. If you're going to splash
out once while in Athens, do it here.
Lyssikratous 4, Plaka.
Tel: (210) 322 7971.

Eden ★★

The oldest vegetarian restaurant in
Athens, with meatless *moussaka* as well
as many traditional meat-free dishes.
Lissiou 12, Plaka. Tel: (210) 324 8858.
Closed: Tue.

Inside an old-fashioned restaurant on Monastiraki

Jimmy and the Fish ★★★★
Frequently cited as the best of the numerous pricey but atmospheric seafood restaurants overlooking the harbour of Mikrolimano.
Akti Koumoundrou 46, Piraeus.
Tel: (210) 412 4417.

Mamacas ★★
One of several trendy new eateries in the up and coming area of Gazi, Mamacas attracts a young, glamorous clientele.
Persefonis 14, Gazi. Tel: (210) 346 4984.

O Platanos ★★★★
Another classic restaurant in the heart of Plaka serving a selection of tasty meat and vegetable stews on an outdoor terrace beneath an enormous plane tree.
Diogenous 4, Plaka. Tel: (210) 322 0666.

Psara's ★★★
Has been serving customers on a series of open-air terraces below the Acropolis since 1898. Live music in winter.
Erehtheos 16 and Erotokritou, Plaka.
Tel: (210) 321 8733.

Athens has elegant traditional restaurants as well as cheeful *tavérnas*

Thanasis ★
Rowdy, cheap and fun. Thanasis offers the city's tastiest *souvlaki* (shish kebabs served with pita bread, salad and chips). *Mitropoleos 69, Monastiraki.*
Tel: (210) 324 4705.

Fish Restaurants
The small fishing harbour of Mikrolimano is surrounded by the best (and most expensive) fish restaurants in Athens.
About 10–15 minutes from the city centre. Take a taxi or the metro to Nea Faliron.

CORINTH
Tavérna O Theodorakis ★★
The best place in Corinth for a slap-up seafood lunch or dinner accompanied by a carafe of house wine.
Seferi 8. Tel: (274) 102 2578.

DELPHI
Tavérna Vakhos ★★
Although Delphi's restaurants are notorious for being expensive and of dubious quality, this family-run *tavérna* is a sound choice. Also affords great views across the Corinthian Gulf.
Apollonos 31. Tel: (226) 508 3186.

IOÁNNINA
Nissi is Ioannina's unforgettable restaurant island. Most are on Monaxon Nektario-Theofanos, a small, tree-shaded *platia*.

Pamvotis ★★★
Possibly the best of a number of outdoor establishments serving freshwater fish and shelfish on Nissi.
Tel: (265) 108 1081.

KALAMBAKA
Panellinio ★
One of the few restaurants in town to stay open all year, Panellinio offers a good choice of hearty soups and barbequed meat dishes in a rustic setting overlooking the fountain on the main square.
Plateia Riga Fereou.
Tel: (243) 202 4735.

MONEMVASÍA
To Kanoni ★★★
Elegant restaurant in a restored 17th-century mansion, overlooking the roofs of the fortified medieval town.
Kástro. Tel: (273) 206 1387.

NAFPLION
Ta Phanari ★★★
Tasty stews such as lamb with okra, moussaka and a good choice of vege-table dishes served up on a vine-covered terrace in this charming seaside town.
Staikopoulos 13. Tel: (275) 20 27141.

PATRAS
Arhontiko ★★
Standing close to the castle, this smart but friendly restaurant offers a good selection of *meze* in an airy dining room from midday onwards.
Germanou 2.
Tel: (261) 062 4834.
Europa Center ★
A perfect choice if you're waiting for a ferry, this informal eatery serves cheap and filling ready-prepared meals overlooking the port.
Othonos-Amalias and Karolou 1, Patra.
Tel: (261) 043 7006.

What to Drink

Beer

Almost all the beers sold in Greece are strong lagers, brewed locally under licence and always served ice-cold. Common brands include Amstel, Henninger, Heineken, Kaiser and Kronenburg, all around 5 per cent alcohol by volume and usually sold in 550ml bottles. Imported beers such as Beck's are often sold in smarter bars, and brands such as Guinness and Newcastle Brown Ale may be found in some resorts. Prices vary widely and depend not so much on what you drink as where you drink it. A small bottle of imported beer in a neon-lit cocktail bar may cost three times as much as a large bottle in a local tavern.

Brandy

Locally made brandy – sometimes described as *koniak* (cognac) – comes in three-, five- and seven-star quality. Sweeter than French brandies, it makes a pleasant after-dinner drink. The best known brands include Cambas and Metaxa.

Coffee and Tea

Kafes elliniko (Greek coffee) comes black and thick, in thimble-sized cups, and is always served with a glass of water. If you like it without sugar ask for *sketo*; if you like extra sugar ask for *glikou*. Most Greeks drink it *metrio*, with one measure of sugar. Instant coffee is universally known as Nes. If you want it hot ask for Nes *zesto* or you may be given *frappe* – iced instant coffee. *Tsai* (tea) is available almost everywhere and is invariably made with British Lipton's

Ouzo comes under many labels, but it always tastes of aniseed

tea-bags. If you like your tea or coffee with milk, ask for it *me gála*.

Imported and Local Spirits

Imported liquors such as Scotch, bourbon, vodka and gin generally cost considerably more than the locally made versions, most of which are destined to be cocktail ingredients. Measures, however, are always generous.

Ouzo

Sunset is the customary time to take your Greek aperitif, though *ouzo* can be (and is) drunk at any hour of the day or night. A clear, sweet, aniseed-based spirit, it is always served with a glass of water and usually with ice. It turns cloudy when water is added.

Retsina

Retsina or 'resinated' wine was formerly stored in earthenware jugs proofed with pine resin, which gave it a distinctive flavour. Today, resin is added artificially. It is an acquired taste, but one worth acquiring, and is by far the cheapest of Greek wines when sold in 550ml bottles.

In many villages the *tavérna* will sell *retsina apo to bareli* (from the barrel) by the carafe and this is always well worth sampling.

Soft Drinks

All the well-known soft-drink brands are available throughout Greece. Although Greek farmers dump surplus oranges by the roadside, freshly-squeezed orange juice (*ximo portokaliou*), available in most holiday resorts, is remarkably expensive.

Tsipouro

A clear and lethal spirit made (like Italian *grappa*) from the skins and pulp left over after pressing grapes to make wine, *tsipouro* is sold in miniature bottles in village *tavérnas* all over the northern mainland.

Wine

Greece makes a range of red, white and dessert wines, all of them affordable and none of them outstanding. In general, white wine (*krasi aspro*) is a better bet than red wine (*krasi mavro*). Boutari, Cambas and Tsantali whites and reds are acceptable. Several small boutique wineries, including Hatzimihali and Lazaridhi, make better and more expensive wines, and are worth sampling if you can find them. Wines maybe categorised as either *ksero* (dry) or *glyko* (sweet).

Greek wines vary, but some of the best come from barrels like these

Hotels and Accommodation

Finding somewhere to stay is almost never a problem in Greece. There is accommodation to suit all pockets in all but the very smallest villages, and even in these you may find the local shopkeeper is willing to rent a spare room (or, in summer, a camp bed in the garden or on the roof). Bear in mind, though, that almost all pensions and hotels in summer holiday resorts close in mid-October and do not reopen until April. You will also find it tricky finding accommodation at Easter (*see pp20–21*) and Apokimisis (*see p19*) when millions of Greeks return to their ancestral villages. Book well ahead for these dates.

Façade of a small hotel in Poros

In theory, Greek accommodation is strictly controlled and licensed by the government. The reality is rather different. Nobody knows exactly how many rooms are available for rent each summer, as local entrepreneurs are continually adding more rooms and apartments, and in practice prices are determined not by the authorities but by market forces. If you turn up before or after the main holiday season you will find hoteliers much more willing to negotiate than in mid-summer. Most accommodation renters will take 10 per cent off the standard rate if you stay for three or more nights.

Accommodation is easy to find. Older hotels, built just before or after World War II, usually cluster around the main square of provincial towns or, in harbour towns, along the waterfront. In smaller villages and resorts, look out for signs offering rooms in privately run accommodation. These usually read 'Rent Rooms' or (for German visitors) '*Zimmer Frei*'. Until the 1980s, such accommodation was usually in the spare bedroom of a family home. These days, it is more likely to be in a purpose-built block with solar-heated hot water and en suite or shared shower and toilet.

In seaside resorts much of the holiday accommodation is in bright, newly built apartments with fully equipped kitchens. These are booked up by holiday companies in high season, but are often available at very reasonable rates in spring and autumn and are excellent value if you plan to stay in one place for a while.

All licensed accommodation is divided into categories starting with L (Luxury) then ranging down from A to E, with separate listings for hotels and for pensions and apartments. Rooms are rated not on quality but on the facilities available (a scruffy old-fashioned hotel with telephones and television in the rooms and a mediocre restaurant will be rated higher than a bright new one without such services). Hotels and pensions are also being built faster than they can be inspected and listed, so many attractive new properties have no rating. The system should be treated with caution. Most accommodation is on a room-only basis, and where breakfast is offered it is rarely worth the €4–6 extra you pay.

Prices vary considerably depending on the season, and can increase by up to 20–30 per cent a year. A twin room with en suite facilities costs from around €30 in a small family-run pension to €300 in a top Athens hotel. A C-class hotel (equivalent to 3-star) cost between €80 and €120. D- and E-class hotels, many of them built between the wars, are usually very cheap and central but shabby and run-down. Few visitors will want to use them.

Most accommodation in seaside resorts closes between the end of October and the beginning of April.

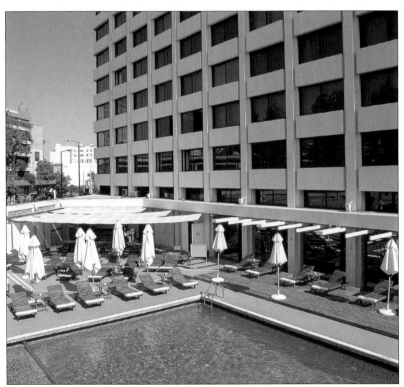

In contrast, the luxurious facilities of the Athenaeum Intercontinental Hotel at Athens

Apartments

Self-catering apartments are available in many holiday resorts, either as part of a package holiday or (in spring and autumn) for independent travellers. They usually have two bedrooms, with a lounge area which can be converted into a third bedroom, and a kitchen equipped with two-ring electric cooker, fridge, pots, pans, glasses, crockery and cutlery.

Campsites

Campsites can be excellent value, especially if you are touring by car. They offer secure parking and camping spaces usually shaded by poplar and plane trees, and facilities usually include a simple restaurant, mini-market, communal showers with constant hot water, and a laundry area. Most campsites are on the coast, next to some of the best beaches in Greece, but there are also sites at places like Olympia and Delphi, many of them with swimming pools. Prices are comparable with the cheapest rooms. Sites to be avoided include those in the Athens area, most of which are unkempt and ill-equipped. A list of campsites in Greece is available from the Greek National Tourist Office or from the **Panhellenic Camping Association** (Solonos 102, Athens; *tel: (210) 362 1560)*.

Hotels

Hotels are classified from A to E, with most A-class properties in the Athens region. C-class hotels, the largest category, are found at all resorts and tend to be big, bland and busy in high season, echoing and empty the rest of the year. D- and E-class hotels, found in larger towns, are cheap but usually grubby and run-down. For a complete list of hotels in Greece contact the **Hellenic Chamber of Hotels** (Stadiou 24, Athens; *tel: 210 323 7193)*.

Pensions

Small, family-run pensions, usually with around a dozen twin-bedded rooms, offer some of the best-value accommodation in Greece, especially off-season. Most of them are recently built, offering rooms with en suite facilities. Solar heating is universal, so do not expect hot water too soon after sunrise.

Staying in Style

The only international-name luxury hotels in mainland Greece are in Athens, most of them close to Platia Syntagma in the city centre or on Leoforos Syngrou. Most have open-air pools as well as business centres, room service, and a choice of expensive restaurants and bars.

Traditional Settlements

The Greek National Tourist Office operates a Traditional Settlements programme which aims to breathe new life into dying communities and to preserve some of the best of Greek vernacular architecture by converting traditionally built homes into comfortable guest-houses, installing modern facilities without changing the style of the building. These are not cheap (rates compare with B- and C-class hotels) but are worth every penny for their atmosphere and location among some of the most spectacular landscapes and most picturesque villages in Greece. There are traditional settlements in the Mani and in Monemvasía in southern Greece, in several of the villages of the Pelion peninsula in Thessaly, and in the Zagória villages in Epirus.

Most provide room-only accommodation. Reservations are essential. Further information from the Greek National Tourist Office (*see p189*).

Village Rooms

In some villages, old-style 'village rooms' are still rented in family homes, where the beds are likely to be elderly and the price may seem disproportionately high. To balance this, you will get a glimpse of local life and as many cups of Greek coffee as you are willing to drink.

Villas

Luxury villas, some with their own pool and landscaped grounds, are available at some up-market resorts such as Vouliagméni on the outskirts of Athens, and are easiest to find as part of a package holiday. Most travel agents should be aware of tour operators offering villa packages.

Youth Hostels

Old-fashioned, crowded, dirty and usually burdened with tyrannical rules and regulations, Greek youth hostels are no cheaper than many privately-rented rooms or older D- and E-class hotels. Many so-called 'youth hostels', especially in Athens, are privately run and have no connection with the International Youth Hostel Association. They are best avoided.

The Grande Bretagne, Athens, lives up to its grand name

On Business

Despite the artificial boost given by European Union cash injections, Greece's economy remains the most problematic in the EU. Privatisation of a cumbersome public sector was suspended with the election of the PASOK government in 1993, and business is burdened by inefficient bureaucracy. Presently even EU citizens who wished to work in Greece required a work permit, and getting it involves touring a number of offices, testing for HIV, and a psychiatric evaluation.

Public phones are conveniently located

Shipping, tourism and agriculture dominate the Greek economy. The shipping industry is in the hands of a relatively small number of private and parastatal companies, but small, family-run operations predominate in farming and tourism.

Many Greek executives are educated in the US, Britain and Canada, and almost all speak fluent English and are familiar with the needs of their overseas colleagues. A new breed of executive sees Europe, rather than the Anglo-Saxon countries, as its role model.

With the collapse of Communism and Soviet influence over its northern Balkan neighbours, Greek business has taken an active interest in the fledgling market-led economies of countries like Bulgaria, Romania, Hungary and even Albania.

Both Athens and Thessaloníki are well positioned to take advantage of shifts in the Balkan business climate, and the Greek government and business community are keen to forge links with the new economies.

Accommodation

Major hotel chains including Hilton International, Inter-Continental, Marriott and Novotel have properties in Athens. The capital's two top hotels, the Grande Bretagne and the George V, are both on Syntagma, the city's central square. Greece's major home-grown hotel groups, Astir Hotels, Capsis Hotels and Elektra Hotels, are the best bet for accommodation in regional business capitals such as Thessaloníki and Patras.

Business Etiquette

Greek business etiquette is relaxed. Punctuality is appreciated, but turning up late for a meeting is not a mortal sin. Normal business wear is jacket and tie for men (a suit is not essential) and skirt or dress for women. Not all Greek offices are air-conditioned, and in summer many executives may dispense with jacket and tie in favour of an open-necked, short-sleeved shirt and slacks. Shake hands on meeting and on parting. Note that many offices close between midday and 4pm.

Business Transport
City to City
Olympic Airways operates an extensive inter-city network. Flights should be reserved before you arrive in Greece as they are often overbooked. Air taxi and helicopter charter services are available from Athens and other major airports. Rapid express trains run between Athens and Thessaloníki (6hr 13min) and Athens and Patras (3hr 26min), but trains to other points are too slow for the business traveller. Inter-city express buses, which are fast, modern and air-conditioned, offer an alternative.

In the City
Taxis are the most convenient way of getting around big cities but finding one unoccupied can be a problem in Athens. Ask your hotel to book a taxi for vital journeys. Car rental is widely available through international and local companies but few business travellers will want to wrestle with the complexities of Greek one-way systems, city traffic and navigation. Chauffeur-driven cars, the best option if within your budget, can be hired through major hotels and car hire companies.

Communications
The Greek telephone system was fully rationalised in 2002. All numbers now have ten digits, including the area code, which you must dial even when within that area.

Conference and Exhibition Facilities
Greece offers extensive facilities for conferences and exhibitions. Accommodation rates for conference and incentive groups visiting outside peak season are very competitive.

The best conference and exhibition venues are in major international hotels, which offer the best communications and back-up services during the event.

Greece's biggest exhibition centre is in Thessaloníki and offers highly professional event organisation and extensive facilities.

Hellexpo (Egnatia 154, 546 36 Thessaloníki; *tel: (231) 029 1111*).

Media
Two English-language newspaprs, *Athens News (www.athensnews.gr)* and *Kathimerini (www.odyssey.gr)*, are useful sources of information for the business traveller. *Athens News* provides a summary of top international stories, reasonable coverage of Greek news and a culture section lisitng forthcoming events in the capital. *Kathimerini (www.ekathimerini.gr)* is a condensed English-language version of the Greek Conservative daily by the same name, giving a run-down of international and national news, and is sold as an insert with the *International Herald Tribune.* The glossy bi-monthly *Odyssey* features amusing and eye-opening stories about Greece and the Greek diaspora. All three are available at most newsstands in Athens.

Secretarial and Translation Services
Bilingual secretarial services and translation facilities can be arranged through the business centres of most leading hotels in Athens and Thessaloníki but are not widely available in smaller cities.

Practical Guide

Arriving
By Air
Athens International Airport is the main gateway for charter and scheduled flights to points throughout Europe and worldwide. Thessaloníki International Airport is the northern gateway. Charter airlines fly to Kalámai (Kalamata) and to Préveza between April and October.

Domestic flights are often overbooked. If you plan to fly within Greece, book your flights before you leave home and remember to reconfirm.

The new Athens international airport, **Eleftherios Venizelos** (*tel: (210) 353 0000; www.aia.gr*) opened in March 2001. It is located 27km (17 miles) northeast of the city, and facilities include blanks, bureaux de change, duty-free shops, bars, restaurants, a post office, a GNTO tourist information office (*tel: (210) 353 0448*), and car hire companies.

The **Athens Urban Transport Organisation** run three 24-hour express bus services linking the airport to the city: line E94 runs to Ethniki Amyna metro station, Line E95 runs to Syntagma Square in the city centre and Line E96 runs to Pireaus Port. Tickets, which cost €2.90, can be bought directly from the driver. Taxi services are also available – the cost is approximately €25 to the city cntre or €30 to Pireaus Port. Some airport taxi drivers will overcharge unwary visitors. Insist that the meter is switched on and check that the figure '1' is illuminated, indicating a normal fare. The figure '2', indicating a double fare, should show only between midnight and 6am or for travel outside the city boundaries, which does not apply to the airport.

By Land
During the 1990s the crisis in the former Yugoslavia cut the most convenient overland route to Greece: this route is now open once more, though train travel is slow and unpredictable. Alternatively, road and rail travellers can use ferries from Italy or travel through Hungary, Romania and Bulgaria.

The monthly *Thomas Cook European Timetable*, gives up-to-date details of most rail and shipping services throughout Europe and will help you plan a rail journey to, from and around Greece. It is available in the UK from some stations, any branch of Thomas Cook or by phoning *00 44 1733 416477*.

In the US contact: SF Travel Publications, 3959 Electric Road, Suite 155, Roanoke, VA 24018 (*tel: 1800 322 3834; www.travelbookstore.com*).

By Sea
Frequent ferries (*www.ferries.gr*) connect Igoumenitsa and Patras with the Italian ports of Ancona, Bari, Trieste, Venice and Brindisi.

Passports and Visas
Passports are required by all except European Union citizens, who may use national identity cards. A maximum stay of six months is permitted. Citizens of

the USA, Canada, Australia and New Zealand may enter for up to 60 days without a visa. Travellers from South Africa will need a visa. Travellers who require visas should obtain them in their country of residence, as it may prove difficult to obtain them elsewhere.

Camping
A list of campsites is available from the Greek National Tourist Office (see p189) and from Panhellenic Camping Association (Solonos 102, 10680 Athens; *tel: (210) 362 1560*). Camping outside official sites is technically illegal, a rule which is widely ignored. (*Also see p176.*)

Children
There are few special facilities for babies or older children except where provided by package tour companies for their clients. Services provided by holiday companies often include babysitting for younger infants, playgroups for toddlers and activity groups for younger children. Baby milk, food and nappies for infants are available in tourist resorts at most mini-markets and elsewhere from the *geniko emporion* (general store) or from pharmacies.

Climate
Winters are mild and short, with temperatures at their lowest (around 10°C, much colder in the mountains) and rainfall at its highest. By March, days are warmer and April and May offer changeable weather with the possibility of rain balanced by the likelihood of sunshine. Rain rarely falls between June and late September.

Midsummer temperatures average more than 30°C. Heatwaves in July and August often bring temperatures of 40°C and above. September temperatures average 25°C and can exceed 30°C.

Weather Conversion Chart
25.4mm = 1 inch
°F = 1.8 x °C + 32

Temperatures drop noticeably through October, but even in December you can often sit outdoors wearing only a light jacket or sweater.

Crime

Visitors are rarely crime victims. Even Greece's big cities are among the world's safest. That said, normal caution should be exercised. Look after money, travellers' cheques, credit cards and other valuables.

Customs Regulations

Normal EU rules apply. Non-EU visitors may bring in 200 cigarettes, 50 cigars or 250g of tobacco, one litre of spirits, two litres of wine or liqueurs, 50ml of perfume and 250ml of cologne.
It is forbidden to export antiquities and works of art found in Greece.

Driving
Accidents

If possible, set up warning signs. In theory, all cars must be equipped with a reflective warning triangle, which not all hire cars are.

If someone is injured, the accident must be reported to the police (*see p183*). Passers-by in such cases are required to stop and assist. It is advisable to contact the police as a precaution, even if the only damage is material.

If you can, write down the names and addresses of other drivers involved, make and licence plates of vehicles, and the names of any witnesses. Write down the date and time of the accident and if possible take photographs from several angles.

Under no circumstances admit liability, sign any statement of responsibility, or lose your temper.

Breakdown

The Automobile and Touring Club of Greece (**ELPA** *www.elpa.gr.*) provides tourist information (*tel: 174*) and road assistance (*tel: 104*), 24 hours a day.

Car Hire

Rental cars are available from international car hire chains in major cities and resorts and from independent local operators. Renting a car in Greece is expensive and you will find it cheaper to make arrangements through an international chain such as Holiday Autos, Budget, Eurodollar, Europcar, Hertz or Avis before leaving home. Rental cars are often over-used and under-maintained – check tyres, brakes and steering before leaving the depot. Full collision damage waiver, personal accident, bail bond and liability insurance is essential.

Even major chains often exclude damage to the underside of the vehicle or the tyres from their collision damage waiver provisions; make sure you have adequate liability insurance for this.

Documentation

A full British or other EU driving licence is valid for driving in Greece. Most other nationalities require an international driving licence. This can be obtained before you leave home or in Greece from the Automobile and Touring Club of Greece (**ELPA**). You will need your national driving licence, passport and a passport-size photograph.

Drink-driving
Blood alcohol content of more than 0.08 per cent is a criminal offence, blood alcohol of between 0.08 and 0.05 per cent a civil offence, and penalties are severe. The best advice is to avoid alcohol altogether when driving.

Fines
Police may impose fines for motoring offences on the spot but may not collect them. The fine must be paid at a Public Treasury office or a bank within 10 days.

Fuel
Petrol costs around the European average. Lead-free fuel is widely available. It is forbidden to carry petrol in a can in the vehicle. Most petrol stations accept credit cards. Petrol stations are not usually self-service.

Navigation, Maps and Road Signs
Romanised spellings of Greek placenames vary. The differences, however, are not so great as to make a name unrecognisable. On main roads, signs are in the Roman alphabet as well as the Greek one. Off the beaten track, signs are often only in Greek, and you will need a working knowledge of the Greek alphabet to find your way (*see* p24).

Rules of the Road
Speed limits (often ignored) are 50kph in built-up areas, 110kph outside built-up areas and 120kph on motorways. Seatbelts must be worn where fitted. You can be fined for not carrying a warning triangle, fire extinguisher and first-aid kit (many rented cars lack these).

Toll Roads
Greece's main toll highway is Odos Ethnikos 1 (National Road 1) between Athens and Thessaloníki, which is overcrowded and under-maintained, with stretches of dual carriageway giving way to stretches of potholed single-track. A second major toll highway connects Athens with Corinth, where it splits, heading south to Tripoli or west to Patras. Tolls are cheap, but unless you are in a hurry the toll roads should be avoided.

Electricity
Voltage is 220 volts AC. You may require an adaptor for the round two-pin sockets in use in Greece. Power cuts are not uncommon.

Embassies and Consulates
Australia Soutsou 37 and Jocha 24, Athens. *Tel: (210) 645 0404;* *www.ausemb.gr*
Canada Gennadiou 4, Athens. *Tel: (210) 727 3400.*
New Zealand Kifissias 268. *Tel: (210) 687 4400.*
United Kingdom Ploutarchou 1, Athens. *Tel: (210) 727 2600, www.british-embassy.gr*
USA Vasilissis Sofias 91, Athens. *Tel: (210) 7212 951/9, www.usisathens.gr*

Emergency Telephone Numbers
Athens
Medical Emergencies *166*
Tourist Police *171*
Fire *199*

Elsewhere in Greece
Ambulance *166*

General Emergency Number *100*
(manned by the police and dealing with crime, fire and medical emergencies).

Health

There are no mandatory vaccination requirements and no recommendations other than to keep tetanus and polio vaccination up to date. Vaccination against hepatitis A and typhoid is also recommended if you intend to travel to some of the remoter areas. AIDS is present. Food and water are safe.

All EU countries have reciprocal arrangements for reclaiming the cost of medical services. UK residents should obtain an E111 from UK post office. Claiming is a laborious and long-drawn-out process and you are only covered for medical care, not for emergency repatriation, holiday cancellation, and so on. You are therefore strongly advised to take out a travel insurance policy to cover all eventualities. You can buy such insurance through branches of Thomas Cook, and most travel agents.

Measurements and Sizes

Greece uses standard European measurements and sizes (*see p185*).

Media

The English-language newspapers *Athens News* (daily) gives a quirky insight into national news and views. The bi-monthly glossy magazine *Odyssey* takes a more thoughtful approach. British, US and European newspapers are on sale in Athens and in most holiday resorts the day after publication. English news bulletins are broadcast daily on the Athens city radio

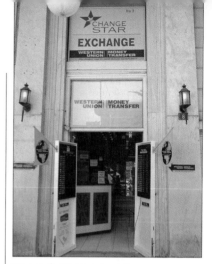

You can change your money here

station (9.84 FM) at 8.30am and 4.30pm. The BBC World Service can be picked up on 107.1 FM.

Money Matters

The Greek currency is the euro (€). Coin denominations include 1, 2, 5, 10, 20, and 50 cents and notes in 10, 20, 50 and 100 euro. Most major currencies, traveller's cheques and Eurocheques can be exchanged at banks, post offices, bureaux de change and travel agencies. The latter two charge a heavier commission but are open when banks and post offices are shut. Banks and post offices are generally open 8am–2pm on weekdays only, but hours may vary.

Credit cards are accepted only in the larger and more expensive hotels, shops and restaurants. MasterCard and VISA are the most widely accepted.

National Holidays

1 January New Year's Day
Variable Epiphany
Variable Shrove Monday
25 March Independence Day

Variable Good Friday
Variable Easter Sunday
Variable Easter Monday
1 May Labour Day
Variable Day of the Holy Spirit
15 August Assumption of the
Virgin Mary
28 October Ochi Day
25 December Christmas Day
26 December St Stephen's Day
See also pp18–21.
Easter and associated moveable feasts are
determined by the Greek Orthodox
calendar. Dates for Easter can differ from
the Western Easter by up to three weeks.

Opening Hours
Banks
See p184.

Museums and Sites
Opening hours given by official sources
often bear little or no relation to those
actually in force at the site or museum,
which may change without notice.
Most sites officially close at 3pm. Some
major sites in Athens stay open longer.
Winter hours for these sites are usually
shorter than summer (1 April to 31
October) hours.

Shops
These are traditionally open from
8am to 1pm and from around 5pm to
8pm. However, shops catering to the
tourist trade usually stay open longer.
Most shops outside tourist areas close
on Sunday.

Organised Tours
Organised tours arranged by travel
agencies in Athens can be an affordable

Conversion Table		
FROM	TO	MULTIPLY BY
Inches	Centimetres	2.54
Feet	Metres	0.3048
Yards	Metres	0.9144
Miles	Kilometres	1.6090
Acres	Hectares	0.4047
Gallons	Litres	4.5460
Ounces	Grams	28.35
Pounds	Grams	453.6
Pounds	Kilograms	0.4536
Tons	Tonnes	1.0160

To convert back, for example from centimetres
to inches, divide by the number in the third
column.

Men's Suits

UK	36	38	40	42	44	46	48
Rest of Europe	46	48	50	52	54	56	58
USA	36	38	40	42	44	46	48

Dress Sizes

UK	8	10	12	14	16	18
France	36	38	40	42	44	46
Italy	38	40	42	44	46	48
Rest of Europe	34	36	38	40	42	44
USA	6	8	10	12	14	16

Men's Shirts

UK	14	14.5	15	15.5	16	16.5	17
Rest of Europe	36	37	38	39/40	41	42	43
USA	14	14.5	15	15.5	16	16.5	17

Men's Shoes

UK	7	7.5	8.5	9.5	10.5	11
Rest of Europe	41	42	43	44	45	46
USA	8	8.5	9.5	10.5	11.5	12

Women's Shoes

UK	4.5	5	5.5	6	6.5	7
Rest of Europe	38	38	39	39	40	41
USA	6	6.5	7	7.5	8	8.5

way of seeing a number of sights outside the city if you have no transport of your own. Drawbacks include those of travelling with a group. Travel agencies and tour operators at popular resorts also offer a range of tours to sights and beauty spots nearby.

Pharmacies

A green cross marks the *farmakio*. Greek chemists have some medical training and can give advice and prescribe medicines for common ailments. Pharmacies open during normal shop hours and are closed on Saturdays and Sundays.

Photography

In November 2001, twelve British and two Dutch plane-spotters were arrested for taking notes and carrying cameras inside a Greek army airbase. They were subsequently imprisoned on spying charges and spent hundreds of thousands of pounds on legal assistance to prove their innocence. In Greece, all military installations are clearly marked with a sign showing 'no cameras'. Be warned that photography and note taking are strictly forbidden!

Places of Worship

Sunday services at most Orthodox churches are held from around 7.30am and last for some hours. Decently dressed (long trousers and shirt sleeves for men, below-the-knee and arm-covering dresses for women) visitors may attend.

Churches of non-Orthodox denominations are found only in Athens, where they include:

The Ireni Metro rail station in Athens

Anglican Church of Áyios Pavlos (St Paul) at Filellinon 29.
Roman Catholic Church of Áyios Dionysios (St Denis) on Omirou.
American Inter-denominational Church of Áyios Andreas (St Andrew) on Sina.

Postal Services

Most larger villages have a post office, distinguished by its prominent circular yellow sign. They are normally open during morning shop hours, but city-centre post offices are also open Saturday mornings. It can often be quicker to change money at a post office than at a bank. Stamps (*grammatosima*) are also sold at kiosks and postcard shops.

Parcels for posting must be inspected by the post office clerk before sealing. Air-mail letters take three to six days to reach the rest of Europe, five to eight days for North America and slightly longer for Australasia. Cards take much longer.

Public Transport
Athens Metro

The Athens metro (*www.ametro.gr*) is being upgraded in preparation for the

2004 Olympics, though building work is
currently behind schedule. There are
now three lines, which operate from
5.30am to midnight. Line 1 runs north-
south between the suburb of Kifissia
and the port at Piraeus. Line 2 currently
runs from Sepolia to Dafni, and should
be extended south to the coastal resort
of Glyfada for 2004. Line 3 runs east-
west from Syntagma Square to Ethniki
Amyna, and should be extended to
Stavros by 2004, from where a new
suburban railway line will run to
Eleftherios Venizelos airport.

Buses

Inter-city buses (www.ktel.org) are
cheap, frequent and fast. Athens has two
long-haul bus stations. Buses for Évvoia
(Evia), Delphi, Ámfissa, Lárisa,
Levádhia, Trikkala and the Metéora go
from Liossion 260. Buses for all other
destinations go from Kifissou 100 (the
best way to reach these bus stations
from the city centre is by taxi).

Municipal buses within Athens and
Thessaloníki display their number and
destination on the front. Tickets can be
bought before boarding from ticket
booths near main stops or from a
periptero kiosk. Stamp your ticket in the
machine by the door on boarding.

Ferries

Piraeus, the port of Athens, is the main
gateway to the Aegean islands
(*www.greekislands.gr*). Many nearby
islands and points on the Peloponnese
coast are served by hydrofoils, some of
which go not from the main Piraeus
harbour but from Zea Marina, about
3km away. Make sure you know where

your boat leaves from. Up-to-date
timetables are published monthly by the
Greek National Tourist Office (*see p189*).
Ferries also sail from Rafína (*see p49*).

Many mainland towns have services
to nearby islands. They include:
Alexandroúpolis (*to Thásos,
Samothráki*).
Astakós (to Itháki, Levkás).
Igoumenítsa (to Corfu, Paxi).
Kavala (to Thásos, Samothráki).
Killíni (to Zákinthos, Kefallinía).
Patras (to Corfu and other Ionian
islands).
Thessaloníki (to Thasos, Samothraki,
Sporades group).
Vólos (to Sporades group).
Yíthion (to Kithira, Andikithira, Crete).
The best guide to this complex system,
with timetable information, is *Greek
Island Hopping*, published by Thomas
Cook Publishing annually.

Taxis

Taxis are cheap and are good value even
for long journeys, especially if you are
travelling with friends. They should be
metered, and most taxi drivers are
friendly, honest and helpful (*see p180* for
possible problems of overcharging).
Drivers may pick up other passengers
going in the same direction: this will not
reduce your fare. In Athens, an empty
taxi is often hard to find.

Trains

Trains are cheap but slow, with the
exception of the express trains between
Athens and Thessaloníki, which take 6
hours 15 minutes. Main routes run
between Athens and Thessaloníki (with
international connections) on the

northern mainland and Athens and Corinth, Patras and Kalamata in the Peloponnese. The most spectacular rail journey in Greece is between Dhiakofton and Kalávrita (*see pp82–3*).

Senior Citizens

Older visitors accustomed to cooler climates may find Greece's fierce midsummer heat unbearable. You may prefer to travel before mid-June or after mid-September, when the weather will be warm but not punishing. Just as Greeks love children, they also respect older people. On the other hand, they also expect them to fend for themselves – for example, when boarding a bus – and in a country where queueing is unknown this can be trying.

Telephones

The easiest way to call is from a metered phone in a street kiosk. You pay at the end of the call. Many shops and small hotels also have metered phones, as do campsites and travel and ticket agencies in resorts. Few of them allow calls using AT&T or similar charge cards. Metered phones are also available in booths at offices of OTE (Greek Telecommunications Organisation). These are cheaper, but hours are less convenient. Dialling codes from Greece are:

Australia *0061*
Canada and the USA *001*
New Zealand *0064*
UK and Ireland *0044*
International Operator *161*

Time

GMT + 2 (+ 3 in summer). Clocks change in spring and autumn on the same date as other EU countries, but the time change does not always coincide with other countries such as the USA.

Tipping

Service is included in restaurants but it is normal to leave small change on the table as an additional tip. This is also usual in bars and cafés. There is no pressure to tip in hotels but a small tip will be welcomed. In taxis, 'keep the change' is normal practice.

Toilets

Standards vary enormously but have improved dramatically in recent years. Toilets in cafés and *tavérnas* are usually better than public facilities. Greek plumbing is narrow-bore and easily blocked, and in most place you are requested not to flush toilet paper but to put it in the waste bin provided. Only the latest modern hotels are exceptions.

Tourist Information

The Greek National Tourist Office (GNTO) has offices worldwide and provides a range of information which includes hotel listings for all parts of the country, up-to-date transport schedules, and information on archaeological sites, exhibitions, festivals, and other events.

Abroad
Australia
51–7 Pitt Street, Sydney NSW 200. *Tel: 00612 9241 1663.*
Canada
91 Scolard Street, 2nd floor, Toronto, Ontario M5R 1G4. *Tel: 001416 968 2220.*
1170 Place du Frere Andre, 3rd floor,

Montreal, Quebec H3B 3C6.
Tel: 001514 871 1535.
United Kingdom
4 Conduit Street, WIS 2DJ London.
Tel: 004420 7495 9300; www.gnto.co.uk
USA
Olympic Tower, 645 Fifth Avenue, Suite
903, New York, NY 10022.
Tel: 001212 421 5777;
www.greektourism.com

In Greece
Athens
7 Tsocha, Ampelokipoi.
Tel: (210) 870 7141; www.gnto.gr
Ioannina
Dodonis 39. *Tel: (265) 104 1868.*
Kalamata
Aristomenous & Polyviou 6.
Tel: (272) 108 6868.
Kavalla
Filellinon 5. *Tel: (251) 023 1653.*
Platia Elefterias. *Tel: (251) 022 2425.*
Komotini
Ap. Souzou 14. *Tel: (253) 107 0996.*

Larissa
Koumoundourou 18.
Tel: (241) 025 0919.
Patras
Filopimenos 26. *Tel: (261) 062 0353.*
Thessaloníki
Georgikis Sxolis Avenue.
Tel: (231) 047 1027.
Volos
Platia Riga Fereou. *Tel: (242) 102 3500.*

Travellers with Disabilities
Facilities for disabled travellers in Greece
are poor. Hotel lifts are often too small
for wheelchairs and ramps are rare.
Pavements – where they exist – are often
uneven. Hilly archaeological sites and
steep village streets and steps pose
special problems. All arrangements
should be checked in advance.
Organisations in the UK which may be
helpful include **Holiday Care** (*tel: 0044
845 1249971; www.holidacare.org.uk*)
and **Tripscope** (*tel: 0044 8457 585641;*
www.tripscope.org.uk).

A quiet moment at the new Eleftherios Venizelou Airport, Athens

ACKNOWLEDGEMENTS

Thomas Cook Publishing wishes to thank the following libraries and associations for their assistance in the preparation of this book.

MARY EVANS PICTURE LIBRARY 14, 15, 56a, 57a, 57b, 62a, 63, 91, 94, 133

ETHEL DAVIES 2, 3, 4a, 9, 12, 20a, 22, 23, 31, 50, 54a, 60, 61a, 61b, 62b, 69, 70b, 90a, 90b, 119, 127, 132a, 134, 135, 136, 138a, 138b, 139a, 139b, 140, 146, 147, 148, 162, 163a, 163b, 164b, 174, 175, 177, 184, 186, 189, back cover top left and cut-out

The remaining pictures including spine, back cover top centre and right are held in the AA PHOTO LIBRARY and were taken by: TERRY HARRIS, with the exception of pages 7, 33b, 34, 36, 37a, 38, 41, 44, 46, 54b, 56-7, 59, 64, 67a, 67b, 68, 72, 75, 89, 124, 141, which were taken by RICHARD SURMAN and pages 18, 150b, 156, 157a, 178 taken by PETER WILSON.

FOR LABURNUM TECHNOLOGIES

Design Director	Alpana Khare	**Photo Editor**	Manju Singhal
Series Director	Razia Grover	**DTP Designer**	Harish Aggarwal
Editors	Madhumadhavi Singh	**CD Editor**	Arfin Zukof
Designer	Neeraj Aggarwal	**CD Designer**	Sudhir Horo

Updating and additional research on this edition was done by Jane Foster.
Thanks to Marie Lorimer for the Index.